THE BIRTHDAY PARTY
and
THE CARETAKER

Text and Performance

RONALD KNOWLES

MACMILLAN EDUCATION

First published 1988

Published by
MACMILLAN EDUCATION LTD
Houndmills, Basingstoke, Hampshire RG21 2XS
and London
Companies and representatives
throughout the world

Typeset by Wessex Typesetters
(Division of The Eastern Press Ltd)
Frome, Somerset

Printed in Hong Kong

British Library Cataloguing in Publication Data
Knowles, Ronald
The birthday party and the caretaker.
—(Text and performance).
1. Pinter, Harold. Birthday Party
2. Pinter, Harold. Caretaker
I. Title II. Series
822'.914   PR6066.I53Z/
ISBN 0–333–42271–6

CONTENTS

Illustrations will be found in Part Two.

ACKNOWLEDGEMENTS

Page references to Pinter's plays are from *Plays: One* (1976) and *Plays: Two* (1977) both published by Eyre Methuen.

I wish to thank the university libraries of Reading, Cardiff and London; Colindale Newspaper Library, the British Library and the British Theatre Association Library. The BBC Transcription Services are thanked for supplying a number of interviews which for convenience have been numbered as follows for reference in the text: Int 1 with Huw Wheldon (5 June 1960); Int 2 with Hallam Tennyson (7 August 1960); Int 3 with Kenneth Tynan (28 October 1960); Int 4 with John Sherwood (3 March 1960); Int 5 with Laurence Kitchin (8 October 1963). Other interviews referred to are Int 6 with Lawrence Bensky in Arthur Ganz (ed.) *Pinter: A Collection of Critical Essays* (1972) and Int 7 with Joan Bakewell *The Listener* (6 November 1969). Reference to the 'Macmillan Casebook' is to *Harold Pinter: The Birthday Party, The Caretaker and The Homecoming* edited by Michael Scott, the editor of this series, whom I must thank for criticism and suggestions. The actress Margery Withers kindly provided information on an early production which is indicated in the text by her name. Doug Pye and Barbara Kidd made available media material and facilities. Lilian Argrave is thanked for her typing skills. Friends and colleagues variously provided London hospitality, encouraged the project and gave moral support. I would like to thank Adrian Clarke, Neil Cornwell, Peter Finch, David Coombs and John Pilling – the last not least for much laughter 'on the Rialto'.

FOR MY CHILDREN
DANIEL AND JESSICA

GENERAL EDITOR'S PREFACE

For many years a mutual suspicion existed between the theatre director and the literary critic of drama. Although in the first half of the century there were important exceptions, such was the rule. A radical change of attitude, however, has taken place over the last thirty years. Critics and directors now increasingly recognise the significance of each other's work and acknowledge their growing awareness of interdependence. Both interpret the same text, but do so according to their different situations and functions. Without the director, the designer and the actor, a play's existence is only partial. They revitalise the text with action, enabling the drama to live fully at each performance. The academic critic investigates the script to elucidate its textual problems, understand its conventions and discover how it operates. He may also propose his view of the work, expounding what he considers to be its significance.

Dramatic texts belong therefore to theatre and to literature. The aim of the 'Text and Performance' series is to achieve a fuller recognition of how both enhance our enjoyment of the play. Each volume follows the same basic pattern. Part One provides a critical introduction to the play under discussion, using the techniques and criteria of the literary critic in examining the manner in which the work operates through language, imagery and action. Part Two takes the enquiry further into the play's theatricality by focusing on selected productions of recent times so as to illustrate points of contrast and comparison in the interpretation of different directors and actors, and to demonstrate how the drama has worked on the modern stage. In this way the series seeks to provide a lively and informative introduction to major plays in their text and performance.

MICHAEL SCOTT

PLOT SYNOPSES

In *The Birthday Party* and especially *The Caretaker* very little happens but a lot takes place. Events are in inverse proportion to the emotional significance of the plays. What takes place in the heart and mind of the characters and audience is the core of dramatic experience here, by which art enlarges our understanding of human need.

The Birthday Party

A scruffily lethargic yet fractious lodger Stanley, seemingly a failed pianist, is the only resident of Meg and Petey's seaside boarding house. Claiming it is his birthday, the fussily maternal landlady presents her lodger with a toy drum. The routine calm is disturbed by the arrival of an outlandish pair, Goldberg and McCann. They appear to know of Stanley, he seems to know of them. A bizarre interrogation implies that he has fled from an organisation which they represent. Fighting is interrupted by the boozy and sentimental party. During a game of blind man's buff, the lights fail, Stanley attacks Meg and Lulu, a guest, and then has a mental breakdown. Next morning Goldberg and McCann take the smartly dressed but speechless Stanley away, and Meg and Petey return to their routine.

The Caretaker

An old Welsh tramp, Davies, is rescued from a fight, after losing his café job, by Aston an ex-mental patient, who takes him back to his squalid attic home. Each are preoccupied with the exigencies of their existence: Davies with getting shoes to go to Sidcup to find his papers; Aston with buying saws to build a shed to repair the house. Aston's brother Mick, a worldly ambitious builder, is less accommodating and sardonically intimidates Davies who nevertheless opportunistically sides with him as the real landlord even though Aston first offers him the job of caretaker. The work-shy Davies eventually turns on Aston who finally joins Mick in rejecting the tramp.

PART ONE: TEXT

1 LIFE AND ART

The genesis of unique works of art can never be entirely accounted for in terms of biography. No series of traceable facts of time and place could amount to a causal aggregate producing a final artistic effect – like a play. Many boys shared a particular London background of the 1930s and 1940s, only one was to write *The Birthday Party* and *The Caretaker*. Yet plays do not spring from some kind of aesthetic vacuum. Directly or indirectly art is related to life and if we glance at the general historical circumstances and the particular milieu of Harold Pinter's early life, distinct features emerge which clearly contributed to the character of his singular artistry.

Pinter was born in 1930, the son of Jewish parents in London's East End. A young Jewish Londoner in the 1930s had a distinct social identity as part of an established community, and in domestic terms Pinter's background was loving and secure. At the same time, with the growth of Fascism and all the paraded brutalism of Mosley's Blackshirt thugs, that identity was an object of anti-Semitic vilification. Within the world of a familiar neighbourhood were those who might, by anything from sarcasm to direct violence, revile Jewishness as foreign and alien. Security and insecurity were side by side. Just outside warmth, care and friendship lay insinuation, abuse and mockery. No other dramatist has so tenaciously recorded modes of sarcasm as Pinter. To be Jewish in such circumstances was to be conscious of oneself as an object of prejudice, of oneself as socially identified and identifiable, and of one's unique individual self, an indefinable subjectivity which fostered detachment and acute observation, the groundwork of art.

Wartime and evacuation saw the extremes of persecution and security. While European Jewry almost perished in the

Holocaust, Pinter was evacuated to the calm, isolated beauty of the Cornwall countryside. Towards the end of the war Pinter had to flee several times from the close ravages of the flying bombs. Leaving the flames behind him, he never forgot to take his cricket bat – pacific emblem of order and security. Postwar London found Pinter, by then a staunch conscientious objector, studying at the Royal Academy of Dramatic Art. However, the overwhelming middle-class confidence of the students proved disorienting. The writer who was, in *The Birthday Party* and *The Caretaker*, to depict the collapse of Stanley and the mental suffering of Aston, then 'faked' a nervous breakdown and left. A significant period followed. Pinter could not bring himself to tell his parents and, as Stanley fantasises on his artistic performances to Meg, so Pinter acted being a student of acting, making up accounts of plays he was supposedly acting in, when in fact he passed time by wandering around London – like Davies of *The Caretaker* and the old women of the sketch *The Black and the White*. 'We're all derelicts' Pinter remarked (Int 1). Yet the self-imposed dereliction of this period was relieved by the close companionship of lasting friendships and regular attendance at Lords cricket ground. Cricket has been a lifetime's passion for Pinter and the dramatic elements of 'play' – competition, attack and defence – within a bipartite structure of repetition, each character/side having its innings 'umpired' by a third party, is characteristic of many of Pinter's plays and particularly *The Caretaker*. (In fact the four characters of *No Man's Land* bear the names of distinguished old cricketers.)

In due course Pinter established himself as a young 'player', touring extensively with Anew McMaster's company in Ireland and then in various repertory companies in England. Again, in another form we find the crucial elements of the foreign and the familiar – here in repertory plays and digs. This is perhaps best brought out by considering the genesis of *The Birthday Party*. Pinter recounted his search for digs, when touring in a farce at Eastbourne one dismal Sunday. Eventually an old deck chair attendant took him to a rather shabby place 'and the whole queer, rather sinister atmosphere remained in his mind until he started writing *The Birthday Party* a year or so ago' (*Daily Telegraph*, 28 April 1958). A letter quoted in an interview forcefully records Pinter's impression of the landlady:

'I have filthy insane digs, a great bulging scrag of a woman with breasts rolling at her belly, an obscene household, cats, dogs, filth, teastrainers, mess, oh bullocks, talk, chat rubbish shit scratch dung poison infantility, deficient order in the upper fretwork, fucking roll on . . .' (Int 6).

The general situation included a curious particular encounter.

> [Pinter] had to share a room with a man in a kind of attic, sleeping in a bed which had a sofa above it. The sofa was upside down, almost against the ceiling, and I was under the sofa, and he was in the other bed . . . and it was all incredibly dirty. And at the end of the week I said to this fellow, who turned out to have been a concert pianist on the pier: 'Why do you stay here?' And he said 'There's nowhere else to go'.   (Int 7)

At the time Pinter was assistant stage manager with the job of operating a horse's head in the farce *A Horse, A Horse* (the interrogation scene of *The Birthday Party* was written in a dressing room at Leicester while acting in *Doctor in the House*). What we have here in the contrast between digs and repertory staple is a curious compound of the familiar made strange. That is to say, a familiar domestic reality of ordinary, mundane associations – unremarkable but for its very drabness – when confronted by someone quite unfamiliar with its privacy who is then immediately included as part of its milieu, appears strange to the point of grotesqueness, as Pinter's letter shows. With the performance of many, if not all, of his plays and certainly with *The Birthday Party*, Pinter puts the audience in his place and we experience the alienation of the familiar. This estranged quality of reality stands in sharp contrast to the stage reality of the repertory theatre with its reliance on the middle-class assurances of reciprocal empathy between audience and actors.

Travelling from town to town over several years, acting in light comedies, thrillers, farces and the like, Pinter must have been increasingly struck by the difference between the process of people's lives as he encountered its blunt unmediated actuality, and the conventional representation on stage of so-called 'reality'. This would have been at its most acute with the question of language. David T. Thompson in his study of

Pinter's repertory background summarises thus: 'dialogue was rarely naturalistic and colloquial but aimed at being selectively respectable and elegant in subject matter and construction' (*Harold Pinter: The Player's Playwright*, p. 72). Could there have been such a clear distinction between the language of life and the language of postwar repertory theatre? In something as representative as, say, J. B. Priestley's *Mr Kettle and Mrs Moon*, which Pinter acted in at Bournemouth in 1956, the language is as clearly articulated as the plot. A rationality of design informs utterance that is a directly functional vehicle for the transparently didactic purpose of the playwright. In contrast, the language of *The Birthday Party* and *The Caretaker* seems relatively inarticulate, illogical and oblique, wandering directionless without the signposts of a plot. For Pinter 'articulate speech' is 'no longer living at all . . . just catch phrases and habitual exchanges of civilised articulate people, which don't possess a living breath of language' (Int 2). But it is not solely a question of middle-class compared to lower-class speech: 'I don't think this kind of dialogue is merely exclusive to working-class people' Pinter told Kenneth Tynan (Int 3).

Looking back over these formative years of Pinter's life we can see many of the characteristic concerns that were to find dramatic expression in his plays. This expression, the core of Pinter's experience and art, is dialectical, including: security and menace, pattern and shapelessness, game and disorder, identity and anonymity, the familiar and the strange, friendship and loneliness. Indeed, through the agency of a close friend, Pinter went from anonymity to celebrity between 1957 and 1960. Though he had written many poems, some of which were published in little magazines, and an unpublished novel, Pinter had not attempted a play until prompted by Henry Woolf, a student at the drama department of Bristol University, which duly produced *The Room* in 1957. The attention of Michael Codron the producer was drawn to this play, he asked to see further work and Pinter sent *The Dumb Waiter* and *The Birthday Party*. Codron promoted Peter Wood's first production of *The Birthday Party* which was in fact quite successful in the provinces before the disastrous one-week venue in London at The Lyric, Hammersmith; the play closed the day before Harold Hobson's *Sunday Times* review appeared resonantly praising Pinter as possessing 'the most original, disturbing and arresting talent in theatrical London' (25 May 1958). However, though deeply discouraged, Pinter was persuaded by the radio drama producer Donald McWhinnie, and other sympathetic BBC personnel, to submit the radio plays *A Slight Ache* (1959) and *A Night Out* (1960). The early plays were now being taken up by theatre companies and then in quick succession *The Birthday Party* and *A Night Out* were broadcast on television in March and April 1960. *The Caretaker* opened at The Arts Theatre Club later in April and was immediately successful, transferring to the Duchess Theatre in the West End where it ran for a year before proceeding to another lengthy run in New York – all to universal acclaim.

As a consequence, Pinter's fame led to a number of interviews, speeches and essays in which he found he was expected to provide some account of his artistry. Pinter is fundamentally an intuitive writer, as will be discussed, and he has no theoretical interest in the nature of writing. Furthermore, because of the resoundingly hostile reception of *The Birthday Party* and the persistently symbolic interpretation of his early plays, Pinter was rather put on the defensive. Nevertheless, discussion of the aesthetic basis of Pinter's early plays is a useful preliminary for both critical interpretation of the text and understanding problems of performance. As an actor, Pinter learnt his 'script', so to speak, for the public presentation of his position, and the same ideas recur again and again.

Pinter's views tend to divide into two: what he is for and what he is against, what he is doing and what he is not doing. Nearly all of Pinter's statements are in reaction to the extreme critical response to his early plays. Some views of *The Caretaker*, for example, dumbfounded the playwright, who considered the play simple and straightforward. Psychological interpretation, on the other hand, explained the play in terms of the conflict between the super ego, the ego and the Id. In the struggle for private property between the owners and the ownerless, Marxists saw the class-war. Alternatively, a theological view allegorised Davies as Everyman, Aston as a Christlike figure and Mick as satanic! 'I wouldn't know a symbol if I saw one' was Pinter's terse response to this kind of thing ('Writing for

Myself', *Plays: Two*, p. 10). In a further comment his position becomes clearer: 'When a character cannot be comfortably defined or understood in terms of the familiar, the tendency is to perch him on a symbolic shelf, out of harm's way' ('Writing for the Theatre', *Plays: One*, p. 11). Rather than clarifying, Pinter sees symbolic interpretation as obfuscatory and intellectually evasive – conceptualising the particularity of a dramatic reality and thus transforming it into an abstraction, the very opposite of its dramatic life. This was made clear by Irving Wardle's comparison in a famous *Encore* essay, 'Comedy of Menace' (September 1958), in which he singles out Nigel Dennis, from a group including Pinter, as the 'arch-abstractionist' whose plays 'are parables that invite you to gaze at a naked theme through the transparencies of plot and character', whereas, in contrast, Pinter's characters possess 'a more complex consistency'.

For Pinter, playwrights like Dennis, starting from an abstract idea or theory, make their characters mouthpieces for their own ideologies, telling the audience what to think – an activity, he felt, more suited to the pulpit, political platform or soapbox. Pinter refrains from giving examples but clearly his strictures would apply to the early work of his contemporaries John Osborne and Arnold Wesker. Moreover, behind any individual lies the powerful dramatic tradition of the *raisonneur*. The *raisonneur*, or 'confidant', is a character who is given information from another leading character, thus functioning as a kind of dramatised mediator between audience and stage, standing in for the normative values of the author. Variations on the figure are found throughout the history of drama and the *raisonneur* became a stock figure of French boulevard theatre of the 19th century and can still be felt vestigially in such 'modern' dramatists as Ibsen and Pirandello. Put simply, Pinter is wholly opposed to the play as a vehicle for the didactic views of the playwright. This anti-didacticism appeared most forcefully in his contribution to a testimonial volume *Beckett at Sixty* in which the terms of his esteem for Samuel Beckett apply equally to his own work, 'I don't want philosophies, tracts, dogmas, creeds, way outs, truths, answers, *nothing from the bargain basement*'.

Hence Pinter's refusal to comply with the request of the first director of *The Birthday Party* for further self-explanatory dialogue for Stanley (Macmillan Casebook). Again, Pinter wished to disassociate his work from that of the contemporary 'kitchen sink' drama. 'I'd say that what goes on in my plays is realistic, but what I'm doing is not realism' ('Writing for Myself', *Plays: Two*, p. 11). Pinter saw his drama as going beyond the imitative aim of duplicating on stage the material reality of environment as appropriate setting for lower-class *mores*, a kind of inverted 'Comedy of manners', a comedy of the mannerless. That 'realism' rests on externals, a surface mimesis. Pinter's 'realistic' is an aspect of a larger reality which compounds external and internal. Implicitly within the tradition of Zola's naturalism, conventional realism sees identity as a natural extension of an environment, as something social. Both identity and environment, for Pinter, are not such solid mutually corroborating things, and reality lies here, precisely with this existential perception. A room cannot question itself, but a human being in a room can and does, but without answer, and that condition is potentially both funny and tragic.

Rejecting the claims of cultural prescription Pinter, like Ionesco, denies the distinctions between tragedy and comedy. The class basis of neo-classical principles of decorum, assigning appropriate character and language to either tragedy or comedy (the noble for tragedy, the peasant for comedy) persisted in various forms until eventually displaced by the development of the realist novel: the portrayal of tragic experience deriving from the heroic idea of knowledge through suffering was displaced by the depiction of social relations governed by the new bourgeois criteria of politeness and elegance. Fate was replaced by the marriage market. Sensation, spectacle and sentimentality deafened and blinded 19th-century audiences to authentic tragedy which became embalmed in imitation, while the heroic and romantic were harnessed together to serve tragic ends in the stately carriage of grand opera, to Brecht the emotional fodder of 'culinary art'. Within an aristocratic culture, classical tragedy had found ideological patronage in the humanism of the Renaissance revival but eventually the democratic element of the liberal and reformist movement of 19th-century society in effect undermined that base. Sensibility rather than suffering characterised the benevolist aesthetic of the late 18th century while Gothic statuary petrified life. In retrospect, Buchner's crazy little soldier *Woyzeck* was more dramatically powerful than all the tragic Goliaths of a Byron or a Schiller. In spite of distinguished plays by such figures as Sean O'Casey, Eugene O'Neill, Garcia Lorca and Arthur Miller, 20th-century theatre is more strongly characterised by tragicomedy, 'black comedy', or *The Theatre of the Absurd* as Martin Esslin's famous study calls it, than by tragedy.

Ionesco felt that 'the comic alone is capable of giving us the strength to bear the tragedy of existence' (Esslin, p. 187). And in case this seems to provide a level of humanist assurance, in *Notes and Counter Notes*, Ionesco went further:

> As the 'comic' is an intuitive perception of the absurd, it seems to me more hopeless than the 'tragic'. The 'comic' offers no escape. I say 'hopeless', but in reality it lies outside the boundaries of hope or despair.   [p. 25]

In comparison Pinter felt that our behaviour is on the edge of absurdity, it is both laughable and yet a source of horror since it verges on the unknown. Clearly this would apply to *The Birthday Party* while early remarks on the traditional genre distinctions indicate the radical dramatic impetus behind such a play as *The Caretaker*. Pinter considered such critical categorisation as facile, arbitrary and stale. 'The old categories of comedy and tragedy and farce are irrelevant' he recorded ('Writing for myself', *Plays: Two*, p. 12). And this reminds us of the great modern master whose ensemble writing deliberately confounds the tragic and the farcical in combining inner suffering with outward buffoonery – Chekhov. Pinter and Chekhov are occasionally compared and indeed in three vital respects, language, silence and laughter, their artistry is quite close.

Chekhov's touchstone was 'life as it is' or, as Pinter put it, not 'the preference for "Life" with a capital L, which is held up to be very different to life with a small l, I mean the life we in fact live' ('Writing for the Theatre', *Plays: One*, pp. 12–13). In Chekhov language is indirect, inarticulate, provisional and suppressed – in spite of occasional outbursts – in reaction to the highly stylised acting tradition of the 19th century with its basis in a rhetorical rather than a psychological use of language. The heritage of classical humanism with its secularised faith in reason and eloquence tended to promote an idealised view of human nature in art, what Man might be, rather than what man in fact is. Pinter and Chekhov are obviously quite out of sympathy with any conventional heroic view of life and art, and any view of language that sustains it. Both recognise the disparity between what is said and what is felt, and the various manifestations in various circumstances this disparity might take. The meaning of any utterance lies not so much in what is said as in the relationship between what is said and what is consciously or unconsciously suppressed but suggested by pause or in silence.

Chekhov's first great director and actor was Constantin Stanislavski who, drawing on his experience of Chekhov's plays, tirelessly theorised on the nature of acting. In reaction to the histrionic posturing of 'star' actors like, for example Sarah Bernhardt (who Chekhov considered a fraud) Stanislavski formulated principles of psychological realism which have dominated acting method in the 20th century. Included here was the fundamental idea of a *subtext* 'the manifest, the inwardly felt expression of a human being in a part, which flows uninterruptedly beneath the words of a text, giving them life and a basis for existing . . . It is the subtext that makes us say the words we do in a play' (*Building a Character*, p. 113). The concept is profound in the existential recognition of the oblique, shifting relationship between being and utterance. Pinter's comparable approach is put rather paradoxically: 'There are two silences. One when no word is spoken. The other when perhaps a torrent of language is being employed. This speech is speaking of a language locked beneath it. That is its continual reference. The speech we hear is an indication of that which we don't hear' ('Writing for the Theatre', *Plays: One*, p. 14). Consider, for example, Stanley's attempt at a conversation with McCann in Act Two of *The Birthday Party*:

You know what? To look at me, I bet you wouldn't think I'd led such a quiet life. The lines on my face, eh? It's the drink. Been drinking a bit down here. But what I mean is . . . you know how it is

. . . away from your own . . . all wrong, of course . . . I'll be all right
when I get back . . . but what I mean is, the way some people look at
me you'd think I was a different person. I suppose I have changed,
but I'm still the same man that I always was. I mean, you wouldn't
think, to look at me, really . . . I mean, not really, that I was the sort
of bloke to cause any trouble, would you? (MCCANN *looks at him*)
Do you know what I mean?

                                             [*Plays: One*, p. 50]

The sense of threat hardly conceals the underlying insecurity
which becomes more and more apparent in the very attempt to
intimidate the morosely imperturbable McCann. Following
the evocation of a life of untouchable respectability, Stanley
attempts to put himself over as a hard-drinking tough-guy. But
in suggesting an alternative personality, Stanley inadvertently
gives voice to the longing for the putative security and stability
of a past identity. The subtextual fear is palpably felt as the
illusions of the past collapse under the threat of the present.
The pretence is recognisably a comic imposture, though Pinter
reminds us '. . . more often than not the speech only *seems* to be
funny – the man in question is actually fighting a battle for his
life' (Int 6).

The aspect of language which Pinter particularly exploits as
playwright is basic communication itself, or rather the
deliberate evasion of communication. Pinter repeatedly
rejected the idea that his plays were concerned with the failure
of communication. He believes rather that we communicate
only too well but evade the full creation of relationship in
articulating that awareness by the evasions of cross-talk,
indirection, changing the subject or affecting incomprehension.
To communicate is to relate and thus to know someone, which
Pinter feels we instinctively evade, fearful of the self-exposure of
mutuality in the vulnerability of reciprocal need. Furthermore,
he feels that the essential conditions of life, socially and
psychologically, work against communication in that it is never
really possible to verify absolutely the given state of things or
indeed what was the case in one's own immediate or distant
past. Thus reality is altogether a precarious set of assumptions
which can be toppled at any time. (In this respect Pinter is often
compared to the Pirandello of *Right You Are If You Think So*.)

Pinter specifically suggested an example of this evasion in the exchanges between Aston and Davies in Act One of *The Caretaker* concerning the woman in the café.

ASTON   You know, I was sitting in a café the other day. I happened to be sitting at the same table as this woman. Well, we started to . . . we started to pick up a bit of a conversation. I don't know . . . about her holiday it was, where she'd been. She'd been down to the south coast. I can't remember where though. Anyway, we were just sitting there, having this bit of a conversation . . . then suddenly she put her hand over to mine . . . and she said, how would you like me to have a look at your body?

DAVIES   Get out of it.
        Pause.

ASTON   Yes. To come out with it just like that, in the middle of this conversation. Struck me as a bit odd.

DAVIES   They've said the same thing to me.

ASTON   Have they?

DAVIES   Women? There's many a time they've come up to me and asked me more or less the same question.

[*Plays: Two*, pp. 33–4]

After another pause the conversation changes direction with the discussion of names. Davies's response to Aston's story evades pursuing whatever particular significance it might have for Aston by implying it is part of women's behaviour in general and thus not at all remarkable. A sense of possibly personal appeal in the revealed intimacy of anecdote as a basis for friendship is thwarted by the impersonal sense of common knowledge, and finally quashed by the farcical improbability of Davies as an object of sexual overtures.

Pinter is the most celebrated writer of comedy in the postwar period, yet the word 'comedy' is inadequate, suggesting as it does an end in itself. Throughout performances of Pinter's plays are found the most memorable occasions of laughter as reviewers have always acknowledged. But when we turn to academic criticism this major aspect of Pinter's art is virtually ignored. That is to say, critics commonly separate performance from meaning. In brief, comedy in Pinter's plays complicates audience response to the surface naturalism by recourse to the theatrical – the inheritance of both classical comedy and popular entertainment. As this comedy precludes easy sentimentality, so it builds up an emotional debt owed to the ultimately serious concerns of this drama. Bernard Dukore has shown that the things we are made to laugh at at the outset have the reverse effect at the close (*Where Laughter Stops. Pinter's Tragicomedy*). This is clearly the case in *The Birthday Party* and *The Caretaker*. (For an extended discussion of laughter in the latter play see my article in the Macmillan Casebook.) However, needless to say Pinter's plays do not develop around a comic line or situation, but from an initial image: one or two people in a room, standing or sitting, and then an entry. Without a blueprint or overall conception, Pinter works from the image intuitively, observing the characters as he observes actual people. And as we might strain to hear an actual nearby conversation, so Pinter strains to hear and record the most appropriate utterance. Image 'engendering' image is the process. The association of these terms, 'image' and 'engender', was repeatedly resorted to in early interviews, recalling Pinter's admiration for W. B. Yeats's poetry by collating lines from 'Byzantium' and 'Leda and the Swan'. 'Those images that yet / Fresh images beget', 'A shudder in the loins engenders there / The broken wall . . .' For Pinter the words are expressive of something organic, like birth, something delivered rather than something fabricated. Sometimes he seems almost to be saying that the playwright is a kind of intuitive recorder rather than an original writer. As if image engendering image were a spontaneous process beyond the will, the character having an autonomy which the writer merely sets in train and then observes. That is to say, Pinter regards his characters as creating themselves outside his mind, quite unlike the kind of stage presence which is no more than a direct embodiment of an idea in the author's mind. This view was expressed most startlingly in Pinter's speech accepting the Hamburg Shakespeare prize.

> It may sound absurd, but I believe I am speaking the truth when I say that I have suffered two kinds of pain through my characters. I have witnessed *their* pain when I am in the act of distorting them, of

falsifying them, and I have witnessed their contempt. I have suf-
fered pain when I have been unable to get to the quick of them . . .

(Theatre Quarterly 1, 1974, p. 4)

Evidently the simple image has an insistent dramatic
potency whereas to some in the audience it seemed that what
ensued was no more than actors following through
improvisatory acting exercises learnt in drama school and
foisted on an innocent public. Reviewing Pinter's own 1964
revival of *The Birthday Party*, Ronald Bryden was reminded of
this elemental nature of the play but saw in the patterns of
domination something essential to acting itself. Domestic
domination finds perfect representation in the histrionic rivalry
of the impromptu, in the extempore immediacy of the given
situation which

> fits the fundamental nature and discipline of the stage. It brings
> back drama to the meaning of the word 'drama': an action,
> something performed before its audience, not merely recollected,
> reported and discussed. It works, as drama-school improvisation
> works: because it uses the actors, confines itself to what they create,
> to what can be seen and felt across the footlights. It is, arguably, the
> essence of the theatre.
>
> *(New Statesman*, 26 June 1964, p. 1004)

The modality of drama is the exact artistic counterpart for that
aspect of life which Pinter wished to explore, 'the living
moment' (Int 4). As an aspiring young writer, Pinter might
well have picked up this phrase from the postwar issues of
Penguin New Writing where it is found introducing the section
devoted to original creative writing, rather than reviews. The
living moment for Pinter is the actual situation itself getting
underway, taking place there and then in particular lives. This
is a specifically existential mode. To render dramatically the
observed process of existence, the stage as the border between
objective and subjective being. 'I want to present living people
to the audience,' Pinter said 'worthy of their interest basically
because they *are*, they exist, not because of any moral the author
may draw from them' (*Times*, 16 November 1959). This
conception has a great dramatic purity, yet reviewers of the

early plays often considered them to be adulterated by 'influence'.

The surprising aspect of Pinter's early reading is that there is no apparent evidence of studying any influential playwright. Pinter is on record as having admired such figures as Hemingway, Dos Passos, Joyce, Dylan Thomas, Auden, George Barker, Henry Miller, Dostoevski, W. B. Yeats and, most famously, Beckett and Kafka. Pinter acted in Shakespeare at school under the inspiring guidance of a much-respected English master, Joseph Brearley, and subsequently acted for nine years in repertory companies. As David T. Thompson has shown, apart from the odd Ibsen or Shaw, these companies were rather conservative, producing nothing from the modernist 20s (Pirandello, Brecht) or postwar avant-garde (Beckett, Ionesco). Before he began writing plays Pinter's knowledge and direct experience of theatre was almost entirely that of conventional mainstream material of the period – more J. B. Priestley than the high priests of modernism. Leslie Smith in a very revealing piece of research (*Modern Drama*, No 4, 1979) found that Pinter had acted in Priestley's *Mr Kettle and Mrs Moon* at Bournemouth and Torquay in 1956. In this play a rebellious bank manager refuses to go to work and as an anti-conventional expression buys some children's toys, including a drumstick which is used on a coal-scuttle, in time to music. Further, Smith points out how a hypnotist-doctor visits the manager who is seemingly brainwashed as he reappears in the banker's uniform of bowler, black coat and pinstripe trousers: Stanley's dress, in fact, at the close of the unrevised first version of *The Birthday Party*. This is not cited to deny the influence of writers like Beckett and Ionesco or the often cited Eliot of *The Family Reunion* and *Sweeney Agonistes* but to indicate that the whole issue of influence is much more ramified than is usually allowed for.

It was on an Irish tour, in 1949, that Pinter picked up an issue of *Irish Writing* and read 'a fragment from Watt' by Samuel Beckett. The experience was shattering and the young Pinter thereafter remained an avid and devoted admirer. Though Pinter must have read and seen *Waiting for Godot* (first English performance 1955 and publication 1956) it was Beckett's prose that absorbed him in the early 50s: 'I didn't read a play of

Beckett's for a long time' he mentioned to Laurence Kitchin (Int 5). Next in importance was Kafka. Of the two Pinter recorded 'When I read them it rang a bell, that's all, within me. I thought something's going on here which is going on in me too.' (Int 5). Kafka with Hemingway is a direct material rather than formal source for *The Dumb Waiter* and *The Birthday Party* and the presence of Beckett can certainly be felt in *The Caretaker*, but the insistent comparisons of Beckett and Ionesco with Pinter's most famous early plays was wildly indulged and became the reviewers' way of evading confronting what made the plays unique.

Hemingway's short story *The Killers* was a direct source for *The Dumb Waiter* and thus has some bearing on *The Birthday Party*. Richard Siodmark extended the story for his film of 1946 starring Burt Lancaster in his debut as the Swede who resigns himself to his end when warned about the hired gunmen who await him in his local café incongruously ordering meals. In Goldberg and McCann's descent on Meg and Petey's household to find their hapless victim in Stanley there are vestiges of the Hemingway story, but here more immersed in the 'genre' situation inherited from gangster films – the hunter and the hunted, avengers and betrayer, hitmen and target. As has always been recognised there is a strong debt to Kafka's *The Trial* in *The Birthday Party*. 'K', Kafka's hero, is summoned on his birthday by two emissaries of unidentified state authority to stand trial for an offence he never discovers. The book ends with K being led to death by his interrogators. In addition to this general outline are several echoes like that of the Advocate's account of legal procedure in Goldberg's bureaucratic account for McCann of procedure in the 'organization'. The influence here is in terms of source material whereas in *The Caretaker*, with *Waiting for Godot* as predecessor, Beckett's influence appears palpably formal. We find structural repetition of theme and language in a total pattern of circularity, the tragicomic or 'absurd' combination of the farcical and the serious, the common tramp figures.

This likeness must be granted, yet at the same time the differences should be weighed in the balance. The texture of each is totally different. Beckett writes in a modernist self-reflexive, metatheatrical mode, an atheist aesthetic mockingly dismantling four centuries of Christian humanism, with intellectual farce tumbling against an exhausted metaphysic. Beckett is avowedly anti-naturalist, while Pinter complicates an exacting naturalism by subjecting it to comic timing. Pinter is a completely non-intellectual, intuitive writer. Behind *Godot* looms the shadow of Descartes, behind *The Caretaker* looms life itself, shades of the dosshouse closing in on Davies. Though Kenneth Tynan saw a general likeness, 'Beckett has undeniably been a great influence on Pinter and the influence is noticeable in Pinter's passionate concern with language as a means of poetic expression', nevertheless he felt that 'Otherwise there is little or no point of contact between their work' (Int 3).

Certain points of contact came up in reviews. The bag-passing game in *The Caretaker* seemed a direct imitation of the hat-swopping routine in *Godot*, and similarly the comic play with shoes in *The Caretaker* was considered as deriving from the preoccupation with boots in *Godot*. However, both Beckett and Pinter inherit and use the repertoire of music hall and vaudeville, the whole phenomena of variety shows combining sketches, stand-up comedians, feed men, monologists, clowns and so on. Of course, Charlie Chaplin stands pre-eminent. Again, the music hall deeply influenced radio comedy and Pinter acknowledged to Michael Billington that in developing his pause-silence technique he was influenced by the American stand-up comedian Jack Benny. We have no need to go to something like Gorki's *The Lower Depths* for the provenance of the likes of Mac Davies. The hobo was a common figure in the early movies and indeed just at the time of *The Caretaker*'s success the highly successful TV series, *The Arthur Haynes Show*, featured Haynes as a cockney worldly-wise tramp with an Irish sidekick, habitually scoring off the middle-class character played by Nicholas Parsons. It might not have turned out quite the same, but *The Caretaker* would have been written without the precedent of *Godot*, since the most powerful influence is life itself as can be found at any time in a walk along the London embankment where Pinter first encountered the prototype of Mac Davies.

The question of Ionesco's influence, insistently affirmed by reviewers of both *The Birthday Party* and *The Caretaker*, might well be partially justified. Ionesco's anarchic, allegorical, surrealistic drama constituted the foremost avant-garde theatre of the 50s. Beginning in a modest back street Paris theatre with *The Bald Primadonna*, Ionesco gradually emerged from art theatres to dominate London's West End in 1960 with *Rhinoceros*, starring Sir Laurence Olivier, only to be outdone in popular success that year by a new young British writer with his play *The Caretaker*. In the 1967 Bensky interview Pinter claimed 'I'd never heard of Ionesco until after I'd written the first few plays'. Yet several years earlier he acknowledged that 'when I wrote *The Birthday Party* I had only seen one of [Ionesco's] plays, *The New Tenant*' (*Times*, 16 November 1959). Presumably this was at the first performance in English at the Arts Theatre Club, November 1956, a year before the composition of *The Room, The Dumb Waiter* and *The Birthday Party*. The formal and stylistic influence on *The Room* is very obvious. In the Ionesco play the old concierge rambles on in garrulous vernacular to the silent new tenant for approximately the first third of the play. The parallel with Rose in *The Room* is very strong. More problematically there is the question of Ionesco's *Victims of Duty*, written 1952, first French performance 1953, first English performance at Dublin 1957. The opening seems very close to that of *The Birthday Party*. Both have a husband and wife in a domestic setting of armchair, newspapers, etc. exchanging small talk (and later there is a comic interrogation reminiscent of that in *The Birthday Party*). Yet John Osborne's *Look Back in Anger* (1956) and N. F. Simpson's *A Resounding Tinkle* (1957) begin in the same way. Pinter has never mentioned Ionesco's play and the coincidences seem striking until we recognise that the newspaper set-up was common as a revue sketch *mise en scène*. The revue sketch is of great importance in understanding a considerable part of Pinter's drama, particularly the early plays, and will be discussed in the following sections on the plays and performance.

2 PLAYS

In considering *The Birthday Party*, *The Caretaker* and other plays of Pinter's early period, one is immediately struck both by the considerable number of common concerns explored in the plays, and by an evident shift in fundamental emphasis. Pinter here works rather like a painter drawn to specific subject matter whose practice is continually to approach his material from different perspectives, with varied groupings, focuses and lights. It is as if, in *The Caretaker*, Pinter had got to the heart of the matter, in its very simplicity recognising the supererogatory and redundant aspects of earlier work. To resort to an oversimplification, realism triumphed over symbolism. Indeed such concerns as self-delusion, insecurity, domination and menace remain constants, but in *The Caretaker* we find an aesthetic resolution, a confident realisation of intuition and creativity meeting in perfect expression, quite freed from the constraints of mannerism.

  This section is accordingly divided into two, looking firstly at *The Birthday Party* and other plays of 1957–59 (*The Room* 1957; *The Dumb Waiter* 1957; *A Slight Ache* 1958; *The Hothouse* 1959), and secondly at *The Caretaker* and other plays of 1959–60 (revue sketches 1959: *A Night Out* 1959). As can be seen from this grouping the revue sketches (particularly 'The Black and White', 'Last to Go' and 'All That') are pivotal in the fullest sense. The plays preceding the revue sketches take particular aspects of that genre as their starting point, whereas the plays that follow embody in developed form what Pinter had learnt in writing such material.

3 *THE BIRTHDAY PARTY* AND OTHER PLAYS 1957–59

The Birthday Party was Pinter's first full-length and most comprehensive early play. It is comprehensive in the sense that it includes most fully in a developed dramatic sense situations, dialogue and techniques of this first group of plays, thereby giving them their most thoroughgoing and memorable expression, as the following brief survey will show.

The Room

The Room is structurally divided into two. The first part consists of Rose's chat to her husband, the unresponsive Bert; the second consists of a succession of visitors – Mr Kidd, the Sands's and the blind Negro Riley. The play is a study in insecurity and as such it is, pretentious as it may sound, a small masterpiece of dramatic phenomenology. Phenomenology rather than psychology since Pinter's artistic concern is not with Rose's mind and what has shaped it, with such questions as causality, motivation and so on, but with the manifestation of a life in the present, as it is in appearance, as it is observed in language and gesture. In this and all of Pinter's plays, being has primacy over character. Unfortunately the dramatic purity of this, as it appears in the first part, is rather crushed by the final heavyweight symbolism of psychic blindness which characterises several of Pinter's early plays, including *The Birthday Party*.

In serving a meal to the silent Bert language and gesture make manifest Rose's being, a condition and a contingency heightened by Bert's imminent departure. Rose's seemingly meandering, nervous, edgy utterance is patterned by a binary subtext. Within her room Rose seems to find warmth, security and companionship removed from the coldness, darkness and loneliness of 'outside'. Her language itself reflects this pattern in the combination of the positiveness of affirmative statements and the negation of subjunctives and questions:

> I don't know why you have to go out. Couldn't you run it down tomorrow? I could put the fire in later. You could sit by the fire. That's what you like, Bert, of an evening. It'll be dark in a minute as well, soon.
>
> [p. 103]

However, the incursions of outside on inside, dark on light, coldness on warmth, the strange on the familiar, begin in the basement – cold, damp, dark and containing the blind Negro Riley.

Riley's entry in part completes the undermining process begun by Bert's seeming dumbness and Mr Kidd's apparent deafness. 'You're all deaf and dumb and blind, the lot of you' [p. 123] Rose cries. But whereas Bert completely failed to respond to her and Mr Kidd failed in part consistently to answer exactly what Rose said, Riley does bring something to her – paradoxically, he is the bearer of identity. The second section of the play is built around a cumulative uncertainty and indeterminacy which culminates in Riley's entry. Beginning with Mr Kidd, Rose is left uncertain about whether he ever had a cleaner, or not; whether the rocking chair was there before, or not; whether Mr Kidd is Jewish, or not. With the entry of the Sands's this insecurity is increased as both the identity of the landlord and Rose's tenancy are called into question. Then the oddity of the Sands's strained behaviour is heightened by the anxious return of Mr Kidd who announces the Negro.

Riley presents an ontological paradox to Rose. The blind Black man symbolises Rose herself, or rather he is an objectification of a condition that she hides from herself. He embodies the foreign, the alien, the bereft and as such he confers existential identity on Rose as 'Sal' on behalf of her 'father'. Not the father of the body, but the progenitor of the mind: her true nature symbolised by the dark and fearful blindness she takes on in a ritual enactment of obeisance and affiliation, touching Riley's eyes and temples before Bert's savage attack on him.

Likenesses to *The Birthday Party* are not hard to find. Above all the common newspaper-sketch theatrical base engrafted on the kitchen-sink naturalism of the set at the opening. Rose and Meg are comparable in the way this process of existence is made manifest in dramatic terms. Obviously the image of the room as a shelter or sanctuary of a putative identity is shared by both plays. Again, the symbolism of sight and blindness reappears in a more integrated way in Stanley's glasses, a motif developed in the film version by William Friedkin. Though *The Birthday Party* uses symbolism it is considerably less arbitrary and contrived than that of *The Room*. It is this that makes the former so unnerving and 'surreal', as it was often labelled. The violence at the close of *The Room* is distanced by the symbolism that precedes it, while in *The Birthday Party* the skilfully mixed modes of the theatrical and the dramatic, the naturalistic and the surreal, the comic and the threatening, never allow the audience to settle into a fixed single response. However, it was with *The Dumb Waiter* that Pinter introduced two more powerful concerns that were eventually to characterise *The Birthday Party* – power struggle and the relation of the individual to some sort of corporate threat. Bert in *The Room* exercises a silent domination, but the power-subservience theme has more a sense of the domestic than the bureaucratic emphasis that is found in *The Dumb Waiter* and *The Birthday Party*.

The Dumb Waiter

Whereas it has been argued that Riley was a symbolic objectification of something within Rose herself, the abstract made concrete, in *The Dumb Waiter* the concrete and the abstract remain separate, providing the dramatic impetus of parallel lines that may meet. Concretely there before us are Gus and Ben whom we eventually learn are gunmen on a job as instructed by 'Wilson' the intermediary for a shadowy 'organization'. Wilson is never seen by us, and the organisation is never identified. Though abstract the proximity of threat makes the organisation very real to those who wait. Ben is in effect the dumb waiter. Dumb in the sense that he does not question the chain of command but simply waits for orders – both aspects travestied by an actual 'dumb waiter' on the wall of the restaurant which bears orders for increasingly exotic dishes. On the other hand Gus indirectly doubts and then directly questions the competence of Wilson which in turn calls into question the efficacy of the organisation itself. As a consequence he becomes the next victim of his partner, Ben. Though Gus's questioning eventually turns on Wilson and the organisation it is himself as functionary that he is no longer certain of, thus his moral defeat immediately before the final tableau, anticipating his murder.

At the outset so much is intimated. Ben reads a bizarre story of an accident to Gus (the newspaper revue base, once again) whose answers provide a catechism of doubt 'He what?. . . No? . . . Go on!. . . Get away . . . Who advised him to do a thing like that? . . . It's unbelievable . . . Incredible.' To Ben 'It's down here in black and white' [p. 130] in the authority of print, a message to be received and accepted, like those he awaits, whereas Gus queries everything. His bed is poor, the basement is windowless, the lavatory cistern malfunctions. But these issues are only oblique diversions for the real question he eventually asks. Why did Ben stop the car on the way to their destination? Gus wishes to understand the nature of things. When they discover the dumb waiter 'BEN *looks into the hatch but not up it*' in contrast to the inquiring Gus who '*leans on the hatch and swiftly looks up*' [pp. 148–9]. Ben is a passive recipient, but Gus enquires further, albeit within his limits, which are quite overcome when he recognises the anomaly of Wilson providing matches when he knew there was no gas. As a functionary Ben, like Goldberg, commands things by commanding words. The cistern fails because of a 'deficient ballcock' [p. 133]; the speaking tube is identified and used, literally a vehicle for orders; Ben will not be intimidated by 'Maccaroni Pastitsio. Ormitha Macarounada' [p. 152], to him, for the purposes of control in a power relationship, they are unequivocally 'Greek dishes' [p. 152]. Thus for Ben the absolute importance of the seeming quibbles on 'light the gas' and 'put on the kettle'; he must confirm the regulative, if not understand the constitutive, correlation between words and things, as part of his position as 'senior partner' within a total bureaucratic structure which must be obeyed because it is infallible. For Gus to be defeated he must be not just shot, but like Stanley unquestioning submission must take the form of impending wordlessness. When the opening dialogue is repeated at the close, Gus's responses are now nullified by the stage directions – *dully . . . very low . . . almost inaudible.*

The Birthday Party

A fundamental critical difficulty presented by *The Birthday Party* is that it does not lend itself to a singular, positivist interpretation. No single formula can encapsulate the plurality of its modes. In fact a deliberate dramatic strategy at work in the play is to promote uncertainty and evasion both onstage and in audience reaction. In its form, matter and performance *The Birthday Party* undermines and subverts responses. The play is a particularly powerful dramatic amalgam in part and as a whole. As a consequence the audience can never settle to a conventional pattern of response. Instead the audience experiences alarming reversals, antithetical shifts and affective contrasts deriving from a uniquely mixed mode. 'Comedy of Menace', 'Theatre of the Absurd', 'Black Comedy' – the journalistic currency of such terms tends to limit rather than open critical discussion. They create a false reassurance by substituting a slogan for thought. In *The Birthday Party* realism of set and naturalism of character are combined with revue sketch material and comic timing: aspects of the gangster thriller are modified by music-hall comedy: Hitchcockian domestic suspense is undermined by farce: a tragic sense is split apart by comic one-liners, while melodrama is subverted by domestic realism (the electric meter runs out!). Pinter does not offer a uniform synthesis of these modes but rather combines them in varying degrees, or juxtaposes one aspect against another to work upon the response of the audience. Audience response is a palpable fact of performance and yet quite problematic as a critical concept, however necessary as a working assumption. Two simplified aspects may be considered: the primary response at an emotional level to the immediacy of the dramatic moment, and the secondary level that is largely retroactive (when we are new to a play) though sometimes simultaneous, by which we begin to recognise a content beyond the affective. This secondary level, which continues beyond performance itself, often displaces the primary response, as indeed text often displaces performance in critical discussion. Examples will make the above points concrete and take us into the work itself.

As Act One opens we seem to be quite emphatically presented with an example of mid-20th-century 'kitchen-sink' realism. The drab living-room of the lower-class household provides the set for the pedestrian opening of breakfast – cornflakes, fried bread, tea and chit-chat. Yet there are clearly

genre associations with the newspaper set-up of the revue
sketch, with the distinctly comic possibilities of distracting
someone from reading. On the one hand we have the
painstaking realism of set and speech apparently there for
purely mimetic ends, on the other we find a theatricality
deriving from the genre situation that undermines an
assimilation of the former.

MEG   What are you reading?
PETEY   Someone's just had a baby.
MEG   Oh, they haven't! Who?
PETEY   Some girl.
MEG   Who, Petey, who?
PETEY   I don't think you'd know her.
MEG   What's her name?
PETEY   Lady Mary Splatt.
MEG   I don't know her.
PETEY   No.
MEG   What is it?
PETEY   (*Studying the paper*) Er – a girl.
MEG   Not a boy?
PETEY   No.
MEG   Oh, what a shame. I'd be sorry. I'd much rather have a
        little boy.

[p. 21]

The comic vacuity of Meg's questioning predisposes the
audience to laughter: we have already heard Petey explain the
difference between light and dark mornings in summer and
winter. Now Meg, as an appropriate adjunct to her darning,
talks with a kind of engaged indifference, the language of habit,
a set of automated impulses triggering questions. The
possibility of laughter is set up in the first question since it is
apparent that Petey is reading a newspaper – one answer to the
question is visibly self-evident. But Petey's response quashes
this by taking the 'what' as referring to the actual news item he
mentions. Meg's next question then releases the laughter that
Petey's reply had contained, in the misplaced affectation of
surprise at the fact of childbirth. Meg's insistence on learning
the name of the mother draws from Petey the music-hall type
eponym 'Lady Mary Splatt'. The incongruously crude

surname jars against the genteel upper-class title. (An extended example from 'Hancock's Half Hour' comes to mind, with the hospitalised Hancock tuning in to 'Woman's Hour', to relieve boredom, only to hear that 'Lady Plunkett will tell us how to fillet haddock'!) Meg's reply provides a comic anticlimax followed by Petey's negative diminuendo which signals comic deflation. Then we have a reversal in the dialogue technique of comic reflation with the further question leading to the renewed laughter of the supererogatory 'Not a boy?'. Yet on the level of secondary response, during the course of the first act, humour is assimilated by a retroactive process which compounds laughter and seriousness thereafter, in recognising the interrelationship of such concerns as childhood, regression and reality in the total structure of the play.

The relationship of public and private, or personal, realities is a major aspect of *The Birthday Party*. The surrender of self through habit to a pseudo-reality is there in the circular structure of the play, returning to morning, breakfast, the newspaper and talk, for Meg, and the consciously suppressed intimations of truth for Petey. As Stanley is clearly a substitute for the child Meg has never had, so the public reality of 'news' is a substitute for the humdrum drabness of immediate experience. This passive homogenisation of events as 'nice bits', to be read out in the newspaper routine, neutralises any real response to actuality, thereby rendering both Meg and ultimately Petey incapable of recognising what had taken place within their own home. McCann's bizarre practice of tearing the newspaper into equal strips is not just a mesmeric piece of stage business. To a certain extent Goldberg and McCann represent a reality of power which burlesques the extremes of the press – domestic sensationalism and sentimentality. Inescapable threat, violence and menace intrude, thus when Petey *'picks up the newspaper and opens it'*, following Stanley's departure *'The strips fall to the floor'* [p. 96]. This political view has recently been endorsed by Pinter himself reappraising his early work in an interview with John Tusa, 'each of the plays, I would say, dealt with the individual at the mercy of an authoritarian system' (*Saturday Review*, BBC 2, 29 September 1985). More specifically, in 1981 Pinter published a rediscovered letter he had written to the first director of *The*

Birthday Party during rehearsals in 1958, evidently in reply to Peter Wood's request for further explanatory dialogue: Goldberg and McCann are 'the hierarchy, the Establishment, the arbiters, the socio-religious monsters [who] arrive to affect alteration and censure upon a member of the club who has discarded responsibility ... towards himself and others' (Macmillan Casebook). Thus the explicit point of Stanley's clothes on re-entry in Act Three in the first production: pinstripe trousers, black jacket, white collar and the bowler hat which Goldberg places on Stanley's head. Though Goldberg and McCann here evidently symbolise the grotesque intimidation of conformity and convention, along with everyone else they are susceptible to psychological escapism in the delusive regression from social reality.

On the public level we see the imposition of abstract authority, while its psychological inversion appears in the regressive movement towards childhood. This takes us to the heart of the play as we recognise the link between authority and childhood – the failure of all father figures. Goldberg's sentimental reverie recalls an idyllic Jewish childhood accompanied by the father figure of Uncle Barney, 'After lunch on Shabbus ... we'd have a little paddle' [p. 37]. Even in marriage Goldberg sees himself as a child by identifying his wife with his mother in the parallel cosseting of gefilte fish and rollmop [pp. 53, 69] and comparing them to Meg, another mother 'My mother was the same. My wife was identical' [p. 81]. As Goldberg was to his mother, so Stanley is to Meg, albeit a mutually slovenly version. 'He's a good boy' [p. 65] Meg says in her birthday speech for which she has given him 'a boy's drum' [p. 46]. When the party gets underway and alcohol begins to take effect the whole group regresses to the point where the children's game of blind man's buff takes over, a collective symbol of their psychological state. Lulu wonders if Goldberg knew her as a little girl. An inversion of Meg, she combines sexuality and girlishness in her need of a father figure, 'I've always liked older men. They can soothe you' [p. 70] she says. McCann, whose 'childish' habit, as Goldberg calls it, is tearing the newspaper, recalls 'Mother' Nolan. Like Goldberg's mother and wife, she fulfilled a reassuring maternal role for one of 'the boys' by serving a meal after a night's drinking. Meg falls into a reverie on the children's home her father sent her to in which nurses and doctors are pathetically transformed into 'Nanny' and 'father'. The attacks on Meg and Lulu by the birthday boy, violent though they appear, are more the simulated enactments of a frustrated angry child who finally giggles hysterically as his discoverers approach.

In *The Birthday Party* characteristics of the father, who combines love and authority, affection and power, are divided and reversed. The personal security of love is displaced by the abstract menace of impersonal authority. This is seen not simply in the words and actions of Goldberg and McCann, but in the image of the failed or absent father. Stanley is let down both at the beginning and at the end of the play. His father did not make the concert at Lower Edmonton and his father-substitute Petey, though he recognises something is going on, fails to prevent Stanley's departure. It appears that Meg's father in effect abandoned her as a child. Now in her sixties she still retains a compensatory fantasy, claiming that the party dress she is wearing was given to her by her father. A father figure is absent from the reverie of McCann to whom Goldberg is the authoritarian replacement, burlesquing Uncle Barney's role by bringing McCann 'down for a few days to the seaside' [p. 37]. Goldberg betrays the childlike trust of Lulu by seduction. Finally, Goldberg invokes the injunctions of his dying father, the Jewish version of middle-class *mores*, to validate his own activity as false father, to make a new man of Stanley in the image of bourgeois society.

Thus it can be seen that the complementary correlatives of the social and domestic, the public and private, the political and psychological, constitute a dialectic from which the play derives its dramatic power.

A Slight Ache

The characters of *A Slight Ache* are quite different from those in Pinter's other early plays where he explores lower-class character, language and milieu. Here the housewife Flora is an ex-Justice of the Peace, while her husband Edward, now a private scholar and proxy squire, was a former polo-playing gentleman athlete. Evidently this is the conservative world of the rural squirearchy (Edward reads *The Daily Telegraph*, naturally). Though the class shift provided the opportunity for stylising upper-class social register, the play contains much of the earlier preoccupations we have seen in *The Birthday Party*. We find the symbolism of failed sight, breakdown, the struggle for domination, the revue sketch base with the opening newspaper and breakfast, and the intruder who brings fear into the room, here the silent tramp-matchseller.

In the original radio production the psychological aspect of the play was much stronger. There, in spite of the sound (if any) of the falling matchbox tray over halfway through, the auditor cannot be entirely sure of the actual presence of the silent matchseller. The tray could be a prop to sustain Edward's projected delusion which Flora at first colludes in and then shares. Stage production, which obviously gives the matchseller a visible presence, partly provides a rational inducement for Edward's disorientation thereby considerably reducing audience tension. The psychological strength of the radio production lay in the dramatisation of an inner reality overwhelming the social reality of the opening, thus emphasising the structure of the play: the collapse of Edward's social and intellectual being and Flora's release of sexual fantasy culminating in her exchanging Edward and the matchseller's identity.

The Hothouse

The Hothouse refers to the malfunctioning radiators of an unidentified mental hospital, which provides a metaphor for the bizarre bureaucratic enclave within the enclosed world of the institution itself. Aston in *The Caretaker* recounts his suffering through electrical treatment in such a place. Rather like the unfortunate Lamb in the play, Pinter himself had volunteered, as a young man, for such treatment 'at ten bob a time' (*Radio Times*, 27 March–2 April 1982, p. 5). Roote, the controller of the institute, could be the counterpart of the shadowy Monty, to whom Goldberg takes Stanley. The victim in *The Hothouse* is the sacrificial Lamb who is blamed for Roote's particular abuse of authority and dies along with all the rest, except the wily Gibbs, Roote's subordinate, who cold-bloodedly allows the inmates to slaughter the administrators. Along with Goldberg and Gus, Roote dramatises one more link in the chain of power and authority, and again like the others, he is found in a situation of dominance and breakdown. As Gus has to handle Ben, and Goldberg McCann, so Roote struggles with the mandarin pedantry of Gibbs. Roote retreats into his office, into himself and into his past, gradually revealing a frightening combination of sentimentality and aggression, self-assertion and obeisance, authority compensating for essential vacuity: the complete Fascist administrator evidently belonging with Goldberg to what we have seen Pinter characterised as 'the heirarchy, the Establishment, the arbiters, the socio-religious monsters . . .'.

Pinter did not allow production of *The Hothouse* until 1980. He considered it too didactic and overtly satirical and its characters as merely cardboard vehicles for the author's point. Although performance was relatively successful on stage and TV the work is not (like *Night School* 1960) as accomplished as Pinter's finest, but its very inequalities bring out the nature of Pinter's dramaturgy. Formally much of *The Hothouse* consists of rather obtrusive revue sketch situations and dialogue and indeed reviewers of *The Birthday Party* and *The Caretaker* often criticised Pinter as no more than a writer of inflated sketches. It is true that much of his work is profoundly influenced by the revue sketch genre, but rather than being a dismissible limitation, it contributed to Pinter's unique aesthetic, as the following section will show.

4 THE CARETAKER AND OTHER PLAYS 1959–60

Revue Sketches

In the period following *The Hothouse*, Pinter wrote a number of sketches for the stage revues *One to Another* ('The Black and

White', 'Trouble in the Works') and *Pieces of Eight* ('Last To Go', 'Request Stop', 'Special Offer'). Other sketches written at this time were subsequently broadcast in early 1964 on the BBC's Third Programme ('That's Your Trouble', 'That's All', 'Applicant', 'Interview', 'Dialogue for Three').

Generally speaking sketches are miniature comedies which entertain through laughter. As such their design often works towards the final punch line which emphasises and confirms the comic impetus, fulfilling audience expectations of the genre. Pinter's 'Trouble in the Works' has this form, adding to the comedy of precise workshop language relocated on stage and subjected to sexual innuendo. Sketches like 'Interview' and 'Applicant' draw on conventional material usually comprising formal or informal encounter in interviews, shops, cafés, rooms, kitchens and so on. 'Applicant' was excerpted from the shelved *Hothouse*, further dialogue of which reappeared as a comic routine in *The Collection* (1961) and as the sketch 'Dialogue for Three'. Indeed the opening of *The Hothouse* is very close to the boss-employee format of 'Trouble in the Works'.

The seriousness with which Pinter regarded his sketches came over strikingly in an early interview where he saw himself as

> a dramatist some of whose work just happens to fit into the framework of a revue. As far as I'm concerned there is no real difference between my sketches and my plays. In both I am interested primarily in people. I want to present living people to the audience, worthy of their interest basically because they *are*, they exist, not because of any moral the author might draw from them.
>
> (*Times*, 16 November 1959)

The particular sketches Pinter had in mind here are 'Last to Go' and 'The Black and White'. To these may be added 'That's All' for the common quality they have which rather separates them from the mere vehicles for laughter. In all three – in the encounter of coffee stall barman with an old newspaper seller, the two old women tramps, and the two housewives of 'That's All' – a realised existential quality is made manifest as an epiphany, a glimpse into a being's mode of existence. The revelation is not that of something unseen, but of seeing and hearing as if for the first time something that has always been before us. It is as if being accustomed to custom and habituated to habit has dulled our response to actuality. By transposing actuality to the theatre and rendering human action and speech in such a minimalist artistic form, our conventionally heightened expectation as spectators is exposed to an existential poverty formalised in slowness and silence. These three sketches, which cannot be quoted without harm, are fragments of fragmentary existence worn smooth in the eddies of repetition and the flux of routine – of days, weeks, months and years. In their simple dramatic purity these little sketches are not only free from the dramatic mechanics of exposition, complication, catastrophe and denouement, but from the characteristic symbolism of the early plays. As we have seen nearly all of Pinter's early plays, and particularly *The Birthday Party*, have the revue format of the newspaper sketch (usually a reader either distracting a second party with news items, or being distracted from the paper) as a creative matrix from which the full play develops. With these three existential sketches it is as if Pinter purged himself of symbolism in preparation for the plays which followed. As Pinter said at the time, he no longer needed to resort to the 'cabaret turns' (Int 4), that *Grand Guignol* of sensationalism which in some ways is burlesqued in *The Caretaker*.

A Night Out

With this play Pinter came closest to contributing to the particular kind of realism which characterised drama on stage, television and film in the late 50s and early 60s. Arnold Wesker's trilogy at the Royal Court Theatre, Pinter's old friend Alan Owen's *No Trams to Lime St* for ABC television and such films as Alan Sillitoe's *Saturday Night and Sunday Morning* all presented the domestic and social realities of lower-class life quite free from the stereotyping comic modes of class-based decorum. In *A Night Out* the ordinary characters are at the centre of the stage, not peripheral attendants on social superiors. Neither are they socially neutralised by any kind of moral idealisation of 'trust' 'devotion' 'honesty' (or the reverse) as such prewar figures habitually were when working-class life had become a kind of costume drama for upper-class actors. Here such massive condescension has gone and actors of the calibre of Tom Bell brought an overwhelming authenticity to the first television audience of sixteen million viewers. Sydney Newman, who came from Canada to produce Armchair Theatre for ABC Television, including *A Night Out*, recorded 'I am proud that I played some part in the recognition that the working man was a fit subject for drama, and not just a comic foil in a play on middle-class manners' (Irene Shubik, *Play for Today*, 1975, p. 40).

Critics have always recognised the close relationship between *The Birthday Party* and *A Night Out*. In the latter, Albert, a mother-dominated, very boyish 28-year-old, is unfairly compromised at an office party, taunted by girls and victimised for his sporting inadequacies by his office senior. In rage and frustration he bullies a shabby-genteel prostitute, the reverse image of his mother to whose emotional blackmail he returns. In both plays Stanley and Albert are haunted by social and sexual failure, both are entrapped by mother figures and both are subjected to the menace of others. However, the fundamental difference between them is that in *A Night Out* everything is determined, definite and identifiable – the bully's malice, the office hierarchy, the mother's possessiveness. In *The Birthday Party* the opposite is the case. As we have seen *The Birthday Party* works on several levels whereas in *A Night Out* there is one constant realist focus. One example will suffice to bring this out. Stanley's musical past is indeterminate. It seems unlikely that he has ever been a concert pianist. Meg's comments are unreliable and precisely what he has been is difficult to identify since we are caught up in Stanley's self-delusion. Without verification we are quite confounded by his social and psychological vagaries. On the other hand, when Albert tells the prostitute that he is an assistant film director we know exactly what is going on. Albert's conscious casual imposture is for him the contemptuous onset of his playful bullying. We recognise this and further identify the inadvertent admission in the glamorous claim of the very dullness of his life. Stripped of symbolism the nagging authenticity of the dialogue is all the more striking. This was one of the features that so impressed the contemporary audience, particularly the discussion of the football match beside a coffee-stall that had provided the setting for the sketch 'Last to Go'.

SEELEY Look. I said to Albert before the kick off, Connor's on the right wing, I said, play your normal game. I told him six times before the kick off.

KEDGE What's the good of him playing his normal game? He's a left half, he's not a left back.

SEELEY Yes, but he's a defensive left half, isn't he? That's why I told him to play his normal game. You don't want to worry about Connor, I said, he's a good ball player but he's not all that good.

KEDGE Oh, he's good, though.

SEELEY No one's denying he's good. But he's not tip-top. You know what I mean?

KEDGE He's fast.

SEELEY He's fast, but he's not that fast, is he?

(pp. 210–11)

This particular dramatic foregrounding of speech was to constitute the primary aesthetic of Pinter's most famous early play which followed, *The Caretaker*, where we find not so much the language of character as the character of language.

The Caretaker

The realism of *The Caretaker* derives primarily from language itself which is not only free from the symbolism and, after revision, the revue sketch elements of the earlier plays, but uninvolved with any real plot or action. Language, character and being are here aspects of each other, made manifest in speech and silence. Character is no longer the clearly perceived entity underlying clarity of articulation, the objectification of a social and moral entelechy but something amorphous and contingent. The language of the play forestalls the dramatic process whereby we assimilate the idea and the fact of human personality, thereby confounding character and being. This may be compared with the black and white photographic studies in Richard Avedon's *In the American West* (1985), 'this silent theatre' as he calls it. Avedon presents us with tramps and various other characters, but in doing so he uses a most arresting technique: the background is removed and the portrait is seen most strikingly against a white ground. As a consequence we are prevented from following through that almost unconscious process by which we respond to a figure as a generic part of a milieu, both mutually conferring an identity that is then familiarly confirmed by us. Here, instead of perception being diffused over a whole area it is now shockingly concentrated on the alarming paradox that what was familiar and recognised generically as a tramp has become estranged and uniquely individual, as if only really seen for the first time.

Pinter has an aural equivalent to Avedon's visual technique and it first appears in a minimalist form in the three sketches discussed above. Speech and silence have a comparable relationship to Avedon's figure and ground. In *The Caretaker* a speaker is seen and heard against a silence. With this arresting immediacy we cannot comfortably place Mac Davies somewhere on a scale of social taxonomy. In the absolute authenticity of his creation he lives, breathes, and is, as we all are. In this respect Davies is not only like Mick and Aston in the sense of failure and isolation, but indeed tends to be a reversed image of ourselves. Pinter remarked that 'We're all derelicts', and what is frightening about Davies is not so much his occasional threats as the fact that his mode of existence inverts the middle-class *mores* of the audience. Davies is partly the image of the secret fears suppressed in a mobile society founded on materialism in which belongings have displaced belonging. Take away our homes and possessions, take away our friends and loved ones, take away our identification with place, and remove the seeming permanence of security and certainty, envisage a decade or so on the roads, and what would we become?

Not only is Davies dispossessed but just before the action of the play starts his single bag of belongings has gone astray. As permanence is an impossible state, so Davies makes the provisional into a permanent condition of his existence: he thanks Aston for 'letting me have a bit of a rest, like . . . for a few minutes' [pp. 19–20]. Likewise Aston's tarring job on the roof will do 'for the time being' [p. 46]. In contrast Mick seemingly has the security of possession, the house itself. In his mock music-hall speeches of Act One Mick evokes the material image of an interconnected familial London with the 'old Mum' at its centre. The humour of the speech itself is a gesture towards class affiliation, a sense of belonging and sharing, while Davies's anecdotes give expression to a peripheral, tangential being – the solitary wanderer only glancing off other lives between Sidcup and Luton. Mick faces Davies with a recognisable identity. To Davies the Blacks, Poles and Greeks are alien. Yet they like Mick have a group social identity. Ironically it is Davies who is the alien.

In what amounts to a burlesque of existential possibility before an entirely contingent world, Davies has just one resource, both comic and desperate, that gives him his only *raison d'être*: choice. Having been thrown out of the café he chooses not to go to Wembley in pursuit of another café job and thus evades a rejection which would confront him with his essential condition. Similarly, he maintains the possibility of going down to Sidcup to retrieve his bureaucratic identity in his papers. As Aston 'might build a shed at the back' [p. 26], so Davies 'might' take up the offer of hospitality 'just till I get myself sorted out' [p. 25]. Davies prefers leather shoes to suede, and turns down those offered by Aston as 'too pointed' [p. 24]: striped shirts are preferred before the checked variety. Mick intuitively divines Davies's character in one word, 'choosy' [p. 40]. The exercise of preference and choice at such a subsistence level is both touching and ludicrous, but pathos is pre-empted by categorical assertion, 'My job's cleaning the floor, clearing up the tables, doing a bit of washing up, nothing to do with taking out buckets!' [p. 18]. By insisting on an imaginary job demarcation Davies invited dismissal. The categorical gives him his only certitude. His Shepherd's Bush mate is not just a public lavatory attendant but presides over 'the best convenience they had' with 'the best soap' [p. 22]. Aston is not just a dreamy do-it-yourselfer *manqué*. For Davies he has to represent the social certainty of 'Carpenter' [p. 26].

Stressed here are some of the qualities which make *The Caretaker* unique, but we do find again aspects in common with *The Birthday Party*: the dominant image of the room and the power struggles between characters: the juxtaposition of the comic and the violent: the threat of bureaucracy. With this last characteristic we can pinpoint the difference between the two plays. The threat of bureaucracy in Goldberg and McCann's 'organization' is Kafkaesque and indeterminate. In *The Caretaker* bureaucracy is solidly expressed in terms of ownership and employment (solicitors and national insurance) regulating society. With Mick, Davies shares a view of identity in terms of social function (landlord, builder, caretaker, carpenter, interior decorator) behind which they hide the recognition of relative personal failure as we shall see in a discussion of performance. Whatever we find in common between the two plays, in *The Caretaker* it contributes to a new whole that does not depend on something like symbolic blindness. *The Caretaker* stands free of such props and indeed suggests to some extent an implicit critique by burlesque of the early plays' violence (the fearsome noisy instrument of Act Two turns out to be an electrolux!). Instead it follows an assured sense of musical composition, the aural displacing the strong visual element of *The Birthday Party* which possesses as Pinter said 'a potent dramatic image and a great deal of this will be visual' (Letter to Peter Wood). Instead of something like the presentation of the drum, the party sequence, the interrogation or the final re-presentation of Stanley, we have the musical sense of exposition, development and recapitulation in the contrapuntal augmentation of shoes, Sidcup and papers: shed, saws and roof. John Mortimer along with many reviewers recognised the musical quality of the first production, praising Donald McWhinnie who 'directed with melodic perfection' (*Evening Standard*, 31 May 1960). In *The Modern Actor* (1973) Michael Billington found that the repetition of 'key nouns' in the Luton speech conveyed 'an almost musical sense of form'. This in fact is found throughout the play. From this point of view Strindberg's *Ghost Sonata* may be seen as a predecessor in its composition which was influenced by sonata form as the title indicates.

Pinter acknowledged an admiration for Webern, and a perceptive early reviewer compared Pinter's sketches with the composer's minimalism. Harrison Birtwhistle is a respected contemporary, while Pinter's selections for his guest appearance on BBC radio's *Desert Island Discs* programme included both Bach and Charlie Parker. In brief, it can be seen that Pinter's musical interests range from the classical to modern serialism and jazz. The combination of the fragmentary and the affective contained by the highly formal is found in the patterned references of Davies and Aston which intertwine in counterpoint, providing a structure that formalises audience emotion, precluding raw sentiment.

The whole design of *The Caretaker* is patterned by repetition of a large number of motifs including such matters as Davies's zenophobia, the bucket, friendship, naming, the Buddha, sleeping arrangements – but the above-mentioned contrapuntal subjects are the most predominant. Pinter's composition allows the concerted preoccupations of Davies and Aston with shoes and shed to alternate in the middle of each act, giving predominance in the first act to Davies with his story of shoe-seeking at Luton and the papers search at Sidcup: Aston's intentions for saws and shed rise to the fore in Act Two, while Davies returns to shoes and Sidcup in Act Three. In addition Pinter places these movements before a fade or blackout thus giving them the effect of melodic augmentation which emotionally culminates in the closing lines of the play (again alternating the close of Act Two where the relation of Aston's past sufferings becomes a present oblation before his shed).

We'll both put up that shed together! [p. 86]

. . . them shoes you give me . . . they're working out all right . . .
. . . if I got down . . . and got my . . . [p. 87]

Both Davies and Aston have circular strategies of survival which necessarily maintain the illusion of progress by means of regress to evade a reality which is all too clear to an audience. As I have put it elsewhere 'For Aston to work on the house he needs to clear the garden for a shed. To build the shed he needs wood. Saws are needed for the wood, a sawbench is needed for sawing, a shed is needed for a sawbench, a cleared garden is needed for the shed. Davies, to sort himself out needs his papers at Sidcup. To get to Sidcup he needs good shoes, to get good shoes he needs money, to get money he needs his papers to sort himself out . . .' (Macmillan Casebook).

PART TWO: PERFORMANCE

5 PRODUCTIONS DISCUSSED

The Birthday Party

1958 at the Lyric Theatre, directed by Peter Wood; Richard Pearson as Stanley; Beatrix Lehmann as Meg; Willoughby Gray as Petey; John Slater as Goldberg; John Stratton as McCann; Wendy Hutchinson as Lulu.

1959 at the Tower Theatre, directed by Kay Gardner; Clyde Jones as Stanley; Margery Withers as Meg; Richard Beale as Petey; Bernard Goldman as Goldberg; David Jones as McCann; Brenda Plumley as Lulu.

1960 ATV production, directed by Joan Kemp Welch; Richard Pearson as Stanley; Margery Withers as Meg; Arthur Hewlett as Petey; Lee Montague as Goldberg; Alfred Burke as McCann; Bernadette Milnes as Lulu.

1964 at the Aldwych Theatre, directed by Harold Pinter; Bryan Pringle as Stanley; Doris Hare as Meg; Newton Blick as Petey; Brewster Mason as Goldberg; Patrick Magee as McCann; Janet Suzman as Lulu.

1968 film, directed by William Friedkin; Robert Shaw as Stanley; Dandy Nichols as Meg; Moultrie Kelsall as Petey; Sydney Tafler as Goldberg; Patrick Magee as McCann; Helen Fraser as Lulu.

1975 at the Shaw Theatre, directed by Kevin Billington; John Alderton as Stanley; Anna Wing as Meg; Basil Lord as Petey; Sydney Tafler as Goldberg; Tony Doyle as McCann; Paula Wilcox as Lulu.

1987 BBC 2 production, directed by Kenneth Ives; Kenneth Cranham as Stanley; Joan Plowright as Meg; Robert Lang as Petey; Harold Pinter as Goldberg; Colin Blakely as McCann; Julie Walters as Lulu.

The Caretaker

1960 at the Arts Theatre Club and Duchess Theatre, directed by Donald McWhinnie; Alan Bates as Mick; Donald Pleasance as Davies; Peter Woodthorpe as Aston.

1964 film, directed by Clive Donner; Alan Bates as Mick; Donald Pleasance as Davies; Robert Shaw as Aston.

1972 at the Mermaid Theatre, directed by Christopher Morahan; John Hurt as Mick; Leonard Rossiter as Davies; Jeremy Kemp as Aston.

1976 at the Shaw Theatre, directed by Kevin Billington; Simon Rouse as Mick; Fulton MacKay as Davies; Roger Lloyd Pack as Aston.

1977 at the Greenwich Theatre, directed by Paul Joyce; Antony Higgins as Mick; Max Wall as Davies; Peter Guinness as Aston.

1980 at the National Theatre (on BBC 1 1981), directed by Kenneth Ives; Jonathan Pryce as Mick; Warren Mitchell as Davies; Kenneth Cranham as Aston.

6   THE PRIMACY OF PERFORMANCE IN PINTER'S PLAYS

Milton's *Samson Agonistes* was written without a performance in mind and Ibsen took great care with the publication of his plays, knowing that they would be read much more as texts than seen as performances. Most playwrights, however, generally write for performance. Why then suggest that performance has a greater primacy in Pinter's drama than in others'? A few broad distinctions might bring us closer to an answer. There are a number of plays which can be considered as drama of ideas. Shaw and Sartre come to mind, for example. Here it could be said that performance illustrates a prior reality, a truth of politics or morality which unfolds and develops dramatising a prior form of propositional knowledge.

Pinter has acted in Sartre's *Huis Clos*, for instance, which dramatically expands the notion that 'hell is other people'. In Charles Marowitz's view the servants of Genet's *The Maids* undergo a transformation in the course of the play: 'We begin to see them as symbols of a writer's idea, and they gain a new credibility. They are no longer real in the sense of identifiable characters from real life but real in the higher sense of characters who personify an idea' (*The Method As Means*, p. 150). This view is then suggested for Goldberg and McCann in *The Birthday Party*. Again, consider the heritage of poetic drama and its greatest proponent. A common lament over Shakespeare's tragedies is that performance so often falls short of the poetry. One of the major developments in modern criticism of Shakespeare was Wilson Knight's post-romantic reading of the plays as highly integrated structures of organic imagery – dramatic poems rather than poetic drama, in fact. However extreme this approach may now be regarded, it has a partial truth. As we have seen, the early plays of Pinter were often considered as vehicles for ideas and Martin Esslin has repeatedly referred to the 'poetic' content of the plays. Yet Pinter's drama remains essentially different from these categories.

If we adapt a few ideas of Plato and Aristotle an aspect of the primacy of performance in these plays becomes apparent. For Plato a play was a lesser reality than what it purported to represent which was itself only an imitation of the transcendental reality of 'ideas' or 'forms'. The intellectual aspect of the drama of ideas may be compared here – the concrete play illustrates an abstract idea. Turning not to Aristotle's counter-argument concerning the universality of poetry in *The Poetics*, but to the underlying principles of his philosophy, we find the means to approach performance. The key ideas in Aristotle are matter and form, potentiality and actuality. For Aristotle the reality of living, changing things is found in the relationship of matter and form. Form is the actuality of a thing, matter is the potentiality for further form. A performance is a living vital thing. As such, in Aristotle's terms, only in performance is meaning made actual in finding form, and further potential form lies in the possibility of other actors, other directors and other performances. Only in performance is

1. *The Birthday Party*, The Lyric, 1958. © Times Newspapers Ltd.

2. *The Birthday Party*, The Shaw Theatre, 1975. © Donald Cooper.

3. *The Birthday Party*, BBC 2, 1987. © BBC.

4. *The Birthday Party*, BBC 2, 1987. © BBC.

5. *The Caretaker*, Arts Theatre, 1960. © Times Newspapers Ltd.

6. *The Caretaker*, Mermaid Theatre, 1972. © Donald Cooper.

7. *The Caretaker*, The National Theatre, 1981. © Donald Cooper.

embodied the greater actuality of form potentially there in the text.

   This is one aspect of the primacy of performance, but it could be applied generally to many other playwrights. With Pinter's drama in particular is the additional all-important relationship of naturalism and theatricality. Only in performance is this fully realised. The theatrical as such can only be properly experienced in the theatre as a fact of performance. Pinter constantly juxtaposes mimetic naturalism with the inheritance of theatrical modes of comedy – farce, revue sketch, cross-talk comedians and so on. A further, complicating factor is that many of Pinter's characters are 'putting on an act'. Actors acting characters acting, in fact. These metatheatrical ironies are realised in performance rather than text, in speech rather than in writing. Further, this is realised as a mode of relationship with each audience, the final consideration of performance. The reality, truth or meaning of a play is in large part founded on the totality of the experience of performance mediated between stage and auditorium, actor and audience. The thoughts and feelings of each auditor are equally part of a play's meaning, but meaning more in the sense of the immediacy of impact (and what it gives rise to) in that precious 'living moment', as Pinter calls it, when embodied existence comes into being, created and apprehended by and in performance.

7 *The Birthday Party*

'They carved me up' [p. 33] Stanley recalls of the concert that failed to take place, and indeed the London critics of the first production of *The Birthday Party* certainly carved up Pinter seeing him as 'the latest recruit to the school of dramatic obscurity' (*Jewish Chronicle*, 23 May 1958), a member of 'the school of random dottiness' (*Financial Times*, 20 May 1958). The *News Chronicle* summarised the play thus: 'The moral would seem to be that every man-jack of us is a raving lunatic'

(20 May 1958). 'Madness' tended to be the most common pejorative for the play. As we have seen Harold Hobson's percipient notice appeared in the *Sunday Times* the day after closure. One week at the Lyric earnt £260, the cheque for which Pinter still keeps framed in his study. To look down from the gallery on a Thursday afternoon matinee to find just six people in the audience and then to read those reviews was a very hard lesson for a new young writer. But the critics' views were sometimes at odds with the rest of the audience's reaction. The *Daily Mail* reviewer 'in fairness' acknowledged of the comic element 'I must record . . . that parts of last night's audience received it with cheers' (20 May 1958). Again, ironically, both before and after the Lyric performance, the play received good notices. As Richard Pearson, the original Stanley, recalled

> We opened in Cambridge and got a terrific reception . . . most people admitted they didn't 'get' the play, but they knew that they had shared a strong emotional experience.
>
> On to Wolverhampton, where they hated it. We felt the audience resented being put through something hair-raising without knowing why. Next, Oxford, and the play was hailed as a minor masterpiece.
>
> (*TV Times*, 18 March 1960)

Michael Simpson's review in *The Isis* (14 May 1958) hailed Pinter as 'a master of suspense' having 'completely assured theatricality'. In fact a number of Oxford students wrote a letter to Harold Hobson 'expressing their dismay at the London reviews' (*Sunday Times*, 15 June 1958). After the Lyric experience the semi-professional cast of the Tavistock Repertory Company put on an inspired performance at the Tower Theatre, Canonbury, which delighted Pinter as Frank O. M. Smith, an official at the theatre, recorded in his memoir: for Pinter this production was '. . . the best there has been and, I am sure, the best there will be of that play. It meant a great deal to me' (*This Insubstantial Pageant*). In particular Margery Withers as Meg so impressed him that he suggested she reappear in the television production, with Richard Pearson, the following year.

Meg, Petey and Lulu

In his seminal lecture on 'Contemporary Drama and Popular Dramatic Forms' (Macmillan Casebook) on Beckett and Pinter, Peter Davison spoke of 'a precarious balance between comic and non-comic' in *The Birthday Party*. In more general terms the precarious balance is between naturalism and theatricality on stage and the different kind of responses they draw from an audience (including the critics). In spite of the precedent of Chekhov with his constant recourse to farce, early critics could not accept the more exaggerated combination in Pinter who was neither a 'straight' realist or farceur. The simplest option was to class him as an absurdist, the intellectual expectations of which preclude an affective response to the play. Pinter's own production of *The Birthday Party* affords a concrete opportunity of assessing that precarious balance in performance.

In the opening exchanges between Meg and Petey, Pinter stressed theatricality with his extremely slow pace which emphasised the revue sketch quality of the scene. Too much so, for Alan Brien, who felt that Newton Blick and Doris Hare 'play all too consciously for the cult-laughter of Pinter fans as if in a revue sketch' (*Sunday Telegraph*, 21 June 1964). Although *The Caretaker* established Pinter's reputation after opening at The Arts Theatre Club on 27 April 1960, televised productions of *The Birthday Party* and *A Night Out* were seen by up to sixteen million people on, respectively, 22 March and 24 April causing a sensation, and Lee Montague's 'indelible' performance as Goldberg, in Robert Ashman's view, 'had a great deal to do with establishing the Pinter vogue' (*Observer*, 19 January 1975). With the 1964 production, audience predisposition toppled the precarious balance Pinter was striving for: 'as each line was greeted with gales of laughter (thus, incidentally, breaking up entirely the text's intricate patterns of rhythm, its assurances and repetitions) one began to wonder if the whole thing had been taken over by the Whitehall', London's leading theatre of farce, as John Russell Taylor recorded (*Plays and Players*, August 1964). Herbert Kretzmer actually specified some of the disrupted moments:

' "What time did you go out this morning?" – *pause* –
"Same time as normal" (*Laughter*) Wife to husband reading paper:
"What's it say?" – *pause* – "Nothing much" (*Prolonged laughter*),
(*Daily Express*, 19 June 1964)

Newton Blick's accent was poor and his presence was 'much
too incisive and stage upper-class'. Doris Hare was 'altogether
too acute for the part; her Meg is not at all the vague, silly,
motherly, sensual bundle of mindless instincts required by the
play' (John Russell Taylor). For Alan Brien they were not
simple-minded enough and projected the consciousness of
comic playing. *The Times* reviewer felt that 'Together they play
the first scene as a cross-talk act, milking it for early laughs . . .
they suggest the bedrock of theatrical cliché which is
continually tripping the production up' which went against the
implicit naturalist criterion of his position: 'The dialogue is
pure improvisation; a method by means of an exact ear for line
lengths, pauses and rhythm, of creating a dramatic situation
from sheerly verbal exercise. Meg and Petey begin as faceless
creatures, handling anonymous language: but by the end of
their duel of clichés they have begun to emerge as recognizable
individuals'. The difficulty lay in recognising and accepting a
mixed response. *The Times* reviewer was responding to one
dimension of the play (implying the incompatibility of its
mixed mode), consequently 'as a result Meg's attachment to
Stanley – instead of being pathetic, absurd, and at moments
inexpressibly touching – declines almost into a coarse joke'. In
contrast Beatrix Lehmann played Meg in the first production
'with touching pathos and frightening realism' (*Plays and
Players*, July 1958). To Bamber Gascoigne, Beatrix Lehmann's
'angular and macabre performance' made such opening
dialogue 'entirely acceptable' whereas 'in the mouth of Doris
Hare's 'plump everyday creature they just sound
unaccountably moronic, and, by implication, very patronising'
(*Observer*, 21 June 1964). Gascoigne's critical premise was that
the characters of *The Birthday Party* were 'a gallery of fascinating
grotesques', yet Pinter had 'tried to make every detail as
ordinary as possible'. Ordinariness characterised the
Tavistock direction of Meg and Petey with 'the . . . feeling of
long-standing and "taken for granted" affection between the

two' (Margery Withers). In contrast R. B. Marriot saw the point of Pinter's direction, 'The relative normality of Meg and her husband Petey . . . finely throws into relief the dark and devious work of the others without the balance of an ordinary, day to day atmosphere being upset. Yet it is one of the triumphs of the play that Meg and Petey can at times appear as outlandish as Goldberg and McCann, and that Goldberg and McCann and Stanley can be as acceptable as if nothing extraordinary were happening to and with them' (*Stage*, 25 June 64).

Pinter's direction exploited the interaction of naturalism and theatricality with their conflicting responses precariously balanced in a particular alienation effect. In the drama of psychological naturalism each member of the audience responds to a state of emotion, of being, in an individual character onstage, whereas the audience as a whole responds collectively to the play as play when unified in the laughter prompted by the theatricality of a comic mode which subsumes character. The dynamism of Pinter's plays derives from this dialectic of performance until finally character triumphs over type. Thus R. B. Marriot in his perceptive and balanced response recognised Doris Hare's 'brilliant quiet intentness never making the basically serious character merely funny'. However, when the play was filmed naturalism was stressed almost entirely.

Although the actors deservedly received superlative praise, the film of *The Birthday Party* had a mixed reception. For John Coleman the 'personal, more hypnotic' quality of the stage contained that opening dialogue of Meg and Petey which seemed parodic without 'the protection of the theatre's immediacy, that special kind of emotional claustrophobia only concentrating on breathing actors in a painted set can provoke' (*New Statesman*, 20 February 1970). *The Spectator* reviewer found an inherent aesthetic tautology, 'Fill the perfectly timed stage pause with a troubled, threatening, domineering close-up and the dialogue becomes mere doubling of a visual statement' (21 February 1970). Commentators in *The Times* (13 February 1970) and *Sight and Sound* (Spring 1970) considered respectively, that 'it loses the rhythm and momentum of a good stage production without establishing any suitable film rhythm' and 'the permanently restless camera destroys Pinter's pauses, his tension and, alas, his humour'. But a positive gain was in 'enclosing us in Pinter's most menacing waking nightmare more completely than a stage production ever could, since we seem physically nearer to it through the camera's eye' (*Guardian*, 12 February 1970). And it should be stressed that one of the great triumphs of the film was the camera work during the Blind Man's Buff game. William Friedkin emphasised the circularity of the opening and closing of the play by continually having the characters circle the table in the middle of the room as tension increases, reaching its height during the game when it is partly shot from above, vertiginously, inducing a palpable nausea and fear. John Coleman felt that the hallucinatory shift from colour to black and white here added to the ghastly impact of it all.

Meg and Petey's boarding house has the terraced solidity of a seaside establishment as the camera, after opening shots of the Worthing promenade, picks up Petey entering after his deckchair labours. The interior is presented by detail with the power of synecdoche as the camera tracks from item to item: in the kitchen a newspaper serves as a tablecloth; the filthy sink is bunged up with tea leaves; the frying pan is blackened and encrusted. On the dining-room table stand a milk bottle, a sauce bottle and an opened bag of sugar – kitchen sink drama indeed. The drabness indicated in Pinter's letter of the 50s describing his Eastbourne digs is faithfully, if not over-emphatically, realised. As Meg goes about her slovenly business she tra-la-la's mindlessly, the sound engineer magnifying the noise of the cutlery as she serves breakfast, tapping the plate with a fork to draw Petey's attention.

The delivery of the opening dialogue was perfectly consistent with this level of material realism. (It was Margery Withers' instinct for the pauses that particularly impressed Pinter in the Tavistock production). Timing, pace and pause was naturalistic rather than theatrical. All the exchanges were low-key and unemphatic, avoiding the comic pitch of the revue sketch. When Petey eventually tells Meg the name of the mother in the newspaper item, 'Lady Mary Splatt', the delivery and reply 'I don't know her' [p. 21] were not timed in a theatrical way to set up comic expectation. On the other hand, the sequence of exchanges in which Goldberg questions Meg about the number of lodgers, including the observation 'And your husband, of course?' [p. 41] received the innocently comic riposte 'Yes, but he sleeps with me'. Delivered naturalistically this fell flat. It demands the comic timing which absorbs the laughter thereby giving Goldberg the cue for the theatrical ploy of picking up 'innocently' where he left off, 'What does he do, your husband?', provoking laughter again.

Dandy Nichols's performance as Meg was a matchless triumph. At no time did she run the risk of patronising the character and no lines were simply played for laughs. The problem here for an actress lies in presenting a character study without resort to a comic performance, when the character is so seemingly empty, without a further dimension to develop. True to the play, Dandy Nichols saw the maternal instinct as the root of Meg's relationship with Stanley. This was brought out not so much in the dialogue as in the accompanying facial expression and head movement. Nothing was overplayed. A possessive toleration was the foundation, as if everything that Stanley might say or do had been said and done before. Thus Meg's gestures were all largely in advance of any answers in their suffocating knowingness. Dandy Nichols used a variety of movements, a knowing loll of the head with raised brows and an affectedly meek smile expressing approbation, censure, pleasure, alarm and so on, but all as if Stanley were a small child with whom she manages in a kind of habitual, patient, exaggerated restraint. In her unremitting consistency and faithfulness to the part Dandy Nichols's assurance triumphed over comedy, caricature and stereotype and presented us with a human being. Limited, unintelligent and irritating but nevertheless an authentic person with a fundamental need at the core of her being – her love for Stanley as the child she wishes him to be. As we have seen, Newton Blick had difficulty with the part of Petey. To Alan Brien the first Petey, Willoughby Gray 'was a stick-figure, a hollow, cardboard creature . . . a newspaper-reading, cornflake consuming automaton' (*New Statesman*, 17 January 1975). It is a limited part and in the film Moultrie Kelsall recognised that to bear with Meg over the years a resigned fatherly forebearance was necessary. In his portrayal it informed every word, gesture and pause.

In Kevin Billington's 1975 production a new dimension was added to Petey, 'Basil Lord gives him a sort of dramatic dignity' consequently his failure was 'almost noble' (Alan Brien). This presentation of Petey had larger implications, as Catherine Itzin saw, 'in Basil Lord's portrayal of him as an intelligent person, the power of terror becomes unbounded. It is one thing to witness violence in an unheeding world, quite another to witness it in a heeding, but helpless one' (*Plays and Players*, March 1975). In addition, another dimension was found in Billington's direction of Anna Wing's Meg who, though 'frumpishly middle-aged and matronly bosom-laden . . . is sensuously sexual as well' (Catherine Itzin). Whereas Margery Withers's portrayal was based on the recognition that '. . . whatever Meg did she did in innocence. Her simple innocence is a vital part of her character'. Presumably Billington took Meg's line 'I've had some lovely afternoons in that room [p. 29] to refer to the recent past with Stanley as sexual partner. In the film Dandy Nichols was more playful than purposeful in her erotic suggestion.

Kenneth Ives's 1987 production for BBC 2 was quite different from the film. Joan Plowright's Meg, unlike Dandy Nichols's sloven, stressed the more lower-middle-class respectability of a landlady whose house is 'on the list', aware of her station as a married woman whom Stanley should duly address aware of his 'place' as lodger. Accordingly Ives's set, though dreary with its dull grey and drab olive, was nevertheless clean and tidy with everything in its place. This Meg kept up appearances. Joan Plowright constantly gesticulated with limp wrists and fluttering hands pointing and touching, so that her ruffling of Stanley's hair and touching the back of his neck were just an irritating extension of her benign fruitiness with constant smile and trifling chuckle. As in Billington's production, Ives stressed the flirtatious sexuality of Meg but she remained a superficial almost abstract presence, unlike the genuine emotional depth Dandy Nichols brought to the part. With her reserved Midlands accent and her wide-eyed credulousness supporting her matronly coiffure, and with Petey's reassurance, Meg reached the final oblivious affirmation of 'I was the belle of the ball . . . I know I was' – in spite of the threat of that wheelbarrow.

Using the full text of 1965 Meg's trepidation about the wheelbarrow in Act Three is restored. Insecurity was the key to Ives's direction. Not just in the central figure of Stanley but the relative insecurity in varying degrees of the other characters, especially Goldberg, as we shall see, and even Petey. The schoolmasterly Petey presented by Robert Lang humoured Meg like a little girl, patiently explaining the difference between light and dark in summer and winter. Here Petey's definiteness and self-assurance was magnified in his challenge to Goldberg and McCann which made the contrast of his final '*broken*' plea extremely telling. Again, by using the full text, Julie Walters's aggrieved Lulu of Act Three was painfully exposed.

'What Goldberg's seduction of Lulu, or her whole character are meant to add I have never understood' (*Observer*, 19 January 1975). Robert Cushman's bewilderment reflects many who have criticised Lulu. A lot of the problem has to do with miscasting. In an early Nottingham Playhouse production, Anne Stallybrass 'struck the right note' as 'horribly normal' (*Plays and Players*, June 1962) whereas Janet Suzman, in Pinter's production, did not 'quite embrace the helpless vacuity' of Lulu (*Sunday Times*, 21 June 1964). For the film Helen Fraser was very well cast, bringing out that pert knowingness and simplemindedness as a sexual counterpart to Meg, but approximately half her dialogue was cut for reasons which will be discussed below. Paula Wilcox in 1975 had 'a sophistication that undermines her credibility' (*Guardian*, 9 January 1975) while to Catherine Itzin her Lulu should have been 'vulgar and as threatening to Stanley as Meg, not petite and pretty and harmless' (*Plays and Players*, March 1975). Though Lulu's character is part of the failed father complex, as we have seen, she is more of a dramatic foil, demonstrating Stanley's sexual failing and Goldberg's sexual prowess, contributing to the rhythm of laughter and apprehension. Yet Kenneth Ives chose to go against this movement at a crucial point, Lulu's re-entry in Act Three. Julie Walters's Merseyside Lulu was so at ease in the part that the 30-year-old dialogue sounded as though it had just been written for her. Frothily inane, this garish coquette giggled through the part. Julie Walters is particularly gifted as a comic actress yet Ives chose to have her final dialogue acted with absolutely straight naturalism. No allowance was made for Lulu's catalogue of comic cliché. Her delivery was determined by the psychology of the abused rather than the comedy of stilted outrage. If this is played up to, Stanley's entry becomes emotionally compromising for an audience which has to go from laughter to silence – a frightening counterpart to Stanley's hysterical state.

Stanley

Richard Pearson established the role of Stanley in 1958 (reappearing in the 1960 ATV production) and tended to remain the standard of comparison until John Alderton's radical reinterpretation of the part in 1975. Commenting on the 'Kafkaesque mystery . . . hinted at with a virtuosity and black humour' of the TV version, *The Times* reviewer added that 'this precise balance between the seen and the hidden . . . needs sympathetic acting, which it certainly received last night, particularly from Mr Richard Pearson' (23 March 1960). In Hutchinson Scott's 'magnificent setting of a decaying Victorian kitchen and mildewed hothouse rolled into one' (*Plays and Players*, July 1958) this Stanley was played 'as the archetypal victim, the fat boy with glasses. He was idle, sweaty, suspicious, edgy and highly sympathetic. This was an intelligent man who looked stupid, partly out of self-defence' (*Observer*, 21 June 1964). Pearson's 'finnicky and falsetto' performance reminded Alan Brien of 'a sluggish, roly-poly Oblomov' (*New Statesman*, 17 January 1975). That set, with the plumpness of Pearson's Stanley, prompted the characterisation 'the Bratbyesque interior' (*Financial Times*, 20 May 1958) recalling the adipose domestic scenes of a leading painter of the 50s.

Harold Pinter's 1964 production at the Aldwych was cast with actors from the Royal Shakespeare Company. In contrast to Pearson's 'soft, rosy and self-indulgent' performance, Bryan Pringle 'won us over' to his image, 'tall, gaunt, awkward, a little waspish, and altogether more of a handful for Meg to smother with concern' (*Plays and Players*, August 1964). However, to Alan Brien 'Richard Pearson's fugitive day-dreamer was a real, spotty, half-blind smelly grub' with a dimension lacking in Pringle's Stanley which was 'too big, too lumpish, too lacking the sly vanity of the self-educated swot' (*Sunday Telegraph*, 21 June 1964). But Pringle's portrayal was not without achievement, drawing duly tempered praise from J. W. Lambert. 'As Stanley, the lost man, Bryan Pringle seems to me to pitch his performance a touch low in the social scale; but there is a strange authority in his confusion, and a world of cruel comedy in his useless protest as he lumbers from side to side of the scene, stretching out his neck like an aggrieved cockney turtle bereft of its shell' (*Sunday Times*, 21 June 1964). The particular difficulty with the part of Stanley is that for the latter half of the second act following the interrogation, with the party and the game of Blind Man's Buff culminating in the onset of breakdown, Stanley has no dialogue. Pinter's direction held back 'from playing the horror aspects all out' (*Plays and Players*, August 1964). As a consequence Pringle's weakness became apparent in this scene as R. B. Marriot witnessed, 'The birthday party itself, macabre, violent, ritualistic, brings the characters into a remarkable union of feeling. This scene, the best in the play, is the least well done in Mr Pinter's production. It lacks tension, and the game of blind man's buff is taken too slowly and deliberately'. The intensity of the interrogation should carry over into the party and give Stanley's silence a sense of horror. The reverse occurred. 'Pringle's Stanley is alive and fascinating in the earlier scenes . . . But as the involvement of the young man with his visitors becomes deeper, and all possibility of escape vanishes Mr Pringle . . . does not carry complete conviction. His silences are only silences: there is little or no sense of what is going on in Stanley, so one is left with a semi-lifeless character in vital passages of the play' (*Stage*, 25 June 1964).

At the heart of the matter, as Peter Hall recounted, was the problem of the director also being the author. The text is the letter. The spirit of a Pinter play is found in performance in the dynamic fluidity of feeling which has to be personally discovered by the actor in collaboration with the director. The actors of the 1964 production took Pinter's remarks 'as God's writ. Therefore they acted results and simplifications . . . however Pinter reacted . . . they took it to be *the answer*'.

Thereafter Pinter resolved 'I'm not going to direct any of my plays again. Not my plays. That's it' (Macmillan Casebook).

Turning to the 1968 film, the presentation of the drum to Stanley provides a comparative focus for three productions discussed so far. Harold Hobson saw Richard Pearson's Stanley as 'a meek little man bitterly hurt when as a birthday present he is given a child's toy drum' (*Sunday Times*, 12 January 1975). In contrast, for Bamber Gascoigne 'when Stanley (Bryan Pringle) unwrapped his present of a toy drum and went round the room beating it, I never once sensed a real person responding ordinarily to this ludicrous and humiliating situation. Instead I saw an actor moving very carefully from half fascinated co-operation to a wild burst of dark fury' (*Observer*, 21 June 1964). Penelope Mortimer found Robert Shaw as Stanley in the film version 'a curious piece of casting, since Shaw is the epitome of the Elizabethan man, competitive, strong, physical', but nevertheless 'it comes off well' (*Observer*, 15 February 1970). Shaw's performance was partly based on his frequent adoption of a register higher than his normal voice. Not so much Pearson's 'falsetto' but at moments a voice emptied of volume – tired, strained and resigned. When Shaw said 'It's a drum. A boy's drum' [p. 46] the tone paradoxically compounded factuality and incredulity as if only at that moment he perceives just what it means to Meg, recognising that the solid reality of the drum makes concrete her maternal fantasies. The force of this recognition made Shaw walk away to the window in humped dismay. Resigned, he then kissed Meg and picked up the drum asking 'Shall I put it round my neck?' Though a question the tone made it a capitulation, the thin-voiced pathos of surrender. Then, in total contrast to Pearson's Stanley, with the drum in position Shaw gave Meg a full smile of acceptance, harbouring no grudge. At this moment it was as if, indeed, the presentation of the drum had brought out the little boy in Stanley, which was emphasised by a little jig as he slowly tapped on the drum in boyish glee. Shortly, the speed and force of the drumming increased as Stanley's face and mouth tightened, his eyes wild, as he drummed frantically, no longer playing an instrument so much as fiercely striking an object – all anticipating the game, regression and violence which follow in Act Two.

To promote the naturalism of the film, Pinter carefully removed Stanley's comic one-liners reminiscent of music-hall patter ('Day-dreaming. All night long' [p. 25]: 'Me. I was in the sea at half past six' [p. 35]: 'I think their policemen are wonderful' [p. 52]). Yet some speeches, uncut, can be delivered theatrically or naturalistically, with different results. Peter Davison argues for comic delivery, with Hancock-like inflation and deflation for most of the dialogue between 'I've . . . er . . . I've been offered a job' to 'All right, Jack, I can take a tip' [pp. 32–3]. Clearly, where we find a sketch-like roll-call of exotic venues 'Constantinople. Zagreb. Vladivostock' along with the centripetal bathos of 'all over the world. All over the country . . . Lower Edmonton' comic possibilities are evident. Yet, as Davison shows, the tone changes to pathos with mention of Stanley's father and the actor favouring theatrical delivery needs a sense of delicate balance, Pinter himself reversing the tone of the following wheelbarrow speech from *low and meaningfully* (1960) to *lightly, casually* (1965). Shaw was intensely naturalistic, consistent with the established realism of set and speech.

In the television production of 1960, Margery Withers recalled that Pearson's Stanley began this speech to delude Meg 'but by the time he had finished he himself was deluded'. In the film when Stanley mentioned the 'job' Shaw's voice was strangely thin and as much addressed to himself as to Meg. The following dialogue, quite different from Davison's comic pacing, was slow and ponderous, not as if Stanley were rehearsing a story, but actually discovering a truth as much for himself as for Meg. Though said in the same tones as 'It's a round the world tour', 'Lower Edmonton' was not funny, but was spoken almost as an aside, taking no comic emphasis. Throughout Stanley's face was serious and slightly pained and his tired voice almost toneless, the words said half-asleep as if the dream were the greater reality. There was no sense of comic imposture, of taking Meg in. There was no audience enlistment against Meg's gullibility. Stanley's face was almost immobile and the deliberate angles of camera and head made it difficult to see Stanley's eyes. This emphasised the feeling of introspection as if Stanley really believed he had been offered a job. What became apparent as the speech progressed was the alarming degree of self-delusion and psychological confusion, altogether more frightening than the stand-up comic delivery, scoring off a dupe. Stanley was here deluding himself, not Meg. What the performance lost in comedy it gained in psychological depth. In spite of this impressive portrayal, when Kevin Billington directed the play in 1975 he provided a radical reinterpretation of Stanley.

John Elsom has stressed the significant contribution Billington has made to the performance of Pinter's plays, he 'has now directed three early Pinter plays; and, in each case, he has refused to dwell upon what used to be regarded as Pinter's distinctive style – the long ambiguous pauses, the hints of distant menace, "the weasel under the cocktail cabinet". If there is a weasel in a Billington production, he is on the dining room table, snarling and biting quite openly' (Macmillan Casebook). Catherine Itzin saw Billington's production as directly opposite to the Peter Hall style, namely 'slow-paced and static, but charged with suppressed emotional energy, precision orchestrated and vibrant with poetic resonance' (*Plays and Players*, March 1975). Quite unlike this, Billington's version 'takes its tone from summer sunshine and a rollicking seaside song . . . Setting and treatment of character is explicitly realistic, not overtly symbolic . . . Menace is concrete rather than vague'. In line with this mode, as Itzin recorded 'John Alderton's Stanley is guilty. He knows it; Goldberg and McCann know that he knows: and we all know that they know that he knows . . . It is to diminish the play to have a Stanley who is a helpless victim. Victim, yes, but guilty and deserving'.

Perhaps Billington took as cue for this interpretation of Stanley's character the fact, often overlooked in criticism, that for all the intimidation of the interrogation, he does fight back. He *kicks* GOLDBERG *in the stomach* as Pinter's stage direction puts it. Bryan Pringle's Stanley puts up only 'feeble resistance' (*Sunday Times*, 21 June 1964), whereas Shaw in the film gives Goldberg a hefty kick in the groin. Alderton's portrayal was of 'a resolutely unsentimental Stan, gruff when he gets the chance, whining when he doesn't' (*Observer*, 19 January 1975). Not the meek little man of Pearson's first performance, here he 'makes the hunt more that of a wary rat than a torpid mouse. His Stanley comes near escaping, if any runaway could, from these modern Eumenides' (*New Statesman*, 17 January 1975). John Alderton generally gained the highest acclaim for 'an extraordinary piece of acting' as Harold Hobson put it (*Sunday Times*, 12 January 1975) but Catherine Itzin felt that the style of the production missed a dimension of the play characterised by Martin Esslin as the view of all that takes place as projections of Stanley's unconscious. There was one moment in the film, otherwise like Billington's production quite realistic, where this expressionistic element came across: towards the close of the interrogation Goldberg and McCann leaned closely in towards the camera (effectively putting the audience in Stanley's place) their faces becoming slightly grotesque and distorted, more like gargoyles embodying cruelly sardonic forces than actual persons. Here Pinter accordingly added dialogue that heightens and then subverts the grotesque by comically secularising the sacred: 'Who hammered in the nails?' asks Goldberg followed by McCann's 'Who drove in the screws?' However, Alan Brien found that John Alderton's performance did work on its own terms 'Yet because he is gruff, sour, selfish and poisonous, his transformation into a white-faced grub, dragged off by waspish predators, is genuinely distressing' (*New Statesman*, 17 January 1975).

Kenneth Ives's production was very fast in pace, very funny and very harrowing. Indeed Kenneth Cranham as Stanley actually looked and sounded increasingly more and more deranged after his first outburst ('Look why don't you get this place cleared! It's a pigsty . . .' [p. 29]). The stage direction here is '*violently*' and Cranham did it full justice. This is important to note since it not only established the emotional pitch but it establishes that Stanley was precariously unstable *before* he hears of, or encounters, Goldberg and McCann who are thus efficient, not material, causes of his collapse. Since Meg's living room is quite tidy it is clear that his vehemence derived from something else. The real danger was made manifest with the presentation of the drum. After turning away from Meg with a nauseous grimace, Cranham returned not to give the kiss she has asked for, but to strangle her. Only at the last moment did he allow his slightly raised arms to drop as his determination left him as – toy drummer now, not concert pianist – he complied with her request.

Though Stanley's first appearance, like all his predecessors was extremely scruffy, Cranham's Franz Liszt-like mane of obviously dyed hair and round gold-rimmed spectacles suggested a bohemian-aesthete manqué who in better times might well have impressed the piano-lovers of Lower Edmonton. This glimpsed reality implied a double escape from a real organisation which had managed to close the second venue. Cranham's delivery of the 'I've been offered a job' exchanges [p. 32] exploited both comic and naturalistic acting styles as if the former actually prompts the latter. The continental excursus was given as a conscious fantasy to take Meg in and to give himself momentary self-importance, but as his boastfulness overtook him in 'All over the country', so it brought to his mind the more limited reality 'I once gave a concert', which thereafter forces the painful recall (however distorted) of a reality. The pain was there in Stanley when Meg finally recalls Goldberg's name just as she has revealed Stanley's name to Goldberg and McCann: camera movement and concentration showed all too clearly that each knew of the other. Again Stanley's conversation with McCann at the opening of Act Two, which ran the whole gamut of emotions from aggressive assertion to craven pleading, carried a very powerful subtext in the stress given by Cranham. The suggestion that came through at intermittent moments was that he remained the same man as he was in the organisation which he had left, without causing any trouble by informing, to hole-up in Basingstoke before, it appears, re-emerging to try to earn a living as pianist eventually 'on the pier'. This ability to suggest concrete happenings and actual situations of the past in the midst of seemingly distraught ramblings, gave Cranham's performance fearful dramatic power which permeated the rest of the act up to that low maniacal laughter. One viewer, at least, momentarily thought that the actor had collapsed under the strain of it all, so unearthly was that sound.

Goldberg and McCann

'Goldberg is, for an actor, the most munificent Jew since Shylock' (*Observer*, 19 January 1975), and Goldberg is set off by

McCann his exact counterpart, clearly deriving from the music-hall tradition, as Bamber Gascoigne recalled of the 1958 production in comparison with Pinter's 1964 revival: 'John Slater's Goldberg and John Stratton's McCann coped better with the zany dialogue because they were more purely the music-hall Jew and Irish man' (*Observer*, 21 June 1964). Similarly, in the 1960 ATV production, Lee Montague and Alfred Burke as Goldberg and McCann 'behaved like cross-talk comedians gone out of their minds' (*Daily Mirror*, 23 March 1960). Altogether 'more stylized', Margery Withers recalls, than the Goldberg and McCann of the Tavistock production. The two characters are particularly reminiscent of Jimmy Jewel and Ben Warris, the postwar cross-talk act. Jewel and Warris, successors to Flanagan and Allen, were unavoidably successful in their popular radio show *Up the Pole* in the late 40s and 50s. Ben Warris with his distinctly Jewish looks, was always sharply dressed in heavily striped suits and was forthright, commanding and aggressive, while Jimmy Jewel (his cousin, in fact) was querulous, complaining and hapless. Warris had a Cockney accent while Jewel as stooge played up his northern voice. Whereas Warris was slightly shorter and sturdily built, Jewel was gangling and gormless. Goldberg and McCann, like Jewel and Warris, also have the contrasted characteristics of the conventional cross-talk act. Goldberg is relaxed, smiling, garrulous and gregarious; McCann is tense, anxious, reticent and introverted. Peter Davison considers that 'Behind Goldberg's description of his Uncle Barney there seems to hover the spirit of that portly comedian, Maxie Bacon' and quoting 'The secret is breathing. Take my tip' [p. 37] dialogue, he recommends that 'This passage, to obtain the music-hall effect, requires to be said in the exaggerated Jewish music-hall fashion' (see Macmillan Casebook).

John Slater threw himself into the music-hall spirit of the part whereas Brewster Mason, directed by Pinter, 'enriches his lines with subtle variations of accent to chime with Goldberg's subtle variations of personality' (*Financial Times*, 19 June 1964). This partly succeeded. In a loud, heavily-striped suit, a visual counterpart to the speech, Mason 'is beautifully in control of the part's bonhomous vulgarity and his relish for the language is a pleasure to share' (*Times*, 19 June 1964) and 'his delivery of the birthday speech throws off the finest piece of vocal coloratura to be heard in the West End' (*Sunday Times*, 21 June 1964). But with Pinter playing down the horror element, Mason 'was more grandiloquent than ghoulish' (*Sunday Telegraph*, 21 June 1964), and 'with remarks like "We all wander on our tod . . .' etc. he seemed 'to be putting on a rather feeble act' (*Observer*, 21 June 1964). As some actresses were patronising in the part of Meg, so Mason impressed as a little too 'upperclassish' for the role of Goldberg. As Clive Barnes put it in a review of a New York production with American actors, 'A man who knows Canvey Island talks about it quite differently from a man who doesn't' (*New York Times*, 4 October 1967).

Patrick Magee first played McCann opposite Harold Pinter himself as Goldberg at Cheltenham in 1960. Cast again in 1964 and then chosen for the film role, he has become as much associated with the part as with that of Krapp in *Krapp's Last Tape*, especially written for him by Beckett. *The Times* reviewer gave the Irish actor an accolade: 'Patrick Magee's McCann, a lantern-jawed ghoul who – as the text requires – can take on the likeness of a thug, a defrocked priest, a brain-washing sadist, and a sentimental Irish drunk. He also has the authority to make an audience accept unexplained actions – such as the bizarre paper-tearing game which last night won two rounds of applause' (19 June 1964). Appearing strikingly in an auburn wig, Magee was 'superbly demonic . . . He . . . gets with a flick of the eyes and a hunch of the shoulders right to the heart of the play. Bland savagery and agonised boredom visibly eat his heart out'. With the song of Act Two Magee's 'terrifying blend of pathos and hatred fuses unforgettably into the stuff of art' (*Sunday Times*, 21 June 1964).

Together Mason and Magee, at their best, on 'their alliance against Stanley, forcing him to stay when he wants to leave, forcing him to sit, their frightful looming threat, their sudden demonstration of brutality . . . are worked out in terms of movement, speech and silence with a thrilling balance' (*Sunday Times*, 21 June 1964). The 'balance' of John Slater and John Stratton's performance was of a different kind from Mason and Magee's which, timed by Pinter's slow pace, almost 'made their playing too psychological' (*Plays and Players*, August 1964) and naturalistic, whereas Slater and Stratton, stressing more that music-hall non-naturalistic backgrounds were 'balanced on a tightrope between burlesque and bizarre' (*Evening Standard*, 20 May 1958). In the film naturalism, as we have seen, was the prevailing mode.

Sydney Tafler was a well-established film actor very familiar to British audiences for his character parts in the postwar cinema as barrow-boy, night-club manager, petty villain and so on. Sharing Pinter's East End Jewish background, he was a perfect choice for Goldberg and his performance in the 1968 film and then in Billington's 1975 stage production crowned his career. To the manner born, Tafler was perfection, particularly so since Goldberg's dialogue has highly specific Jewish speech rhythms. Yet Tafler had the gift of sustaining absolutely precise enunciation. In a word, Tafler's Goldberg was completely and utterly natural. A non-Jewish actor could never have done what Tafler did with hand movements throughout the film, but never obtrusively: so many gestures to emphasise or intensify – to persuade, to reveal, to share, to acknowledge, to challenge, to question, to cajole. The natural virtuosity was endless. Yet the very naturalness deprived the part of most of its larger than life quality, the sense in which Goldberg projects Jewishness in a gentile milieu both to expose and conceal, to masquerade and to deride. A non-Jewish actor, like John Slater or Brewster Mason, given the exaggerated quality of Goldberg himself, almost inevitably inclines towards the stereotype, bringing out, as we have seen, the music-hall provenance. Solto, in *Night School* (1960) uses conventional music-hall wordplay ('A Lascar . . . Alaska?', p. 212), in a comparable Jewish bravura part which Pinter acknowledged was overwritten. Accordingly, whereas the 1964 costume designer gave Mason that impressively smart, heavily-striped suit very reminiscent of Ben Warris (still performing with Jewel as late as 1967), in the film Tafler was smartly dressed in sober, restrained clothes, entering and leaving in a dark suit, similarly accompanied by Stanley, no longer the city gent of the first productions.

This fundamental issue of Goldberg's presentation is perhaps best seen by considering the textual excisions (and slight additions) between 1958 and 1968. After directing the 1964 Aldwych production, Pinter published a revised text in

1965. Most of the cuts concerning Goldberg and McCann
occur towards the close of Act 3. McCann's qualms about
Lulu's nightmares and Goldberg's reply that they were merely
singing, is cut. Then goes bizarre stage business and dialogue
with McCann examining Goldberg's throat with a spoon after
Goldberg has emitted an alarming '*high-pitched wheeze-whine*'
followed by his vigorous exercise with a chest-expander which
breaks under the strain. Lastly part of the music-hall exchanges
between Goldberg and Lulu are excised. Clearly Pinter
recognised that talk of nightmare, alarming sounds and
slapstick gestures all detracted from the dramatic power of
Stanley's fearful re-entry and his subsequent ghastly sounds.
With the film version the cuts were increased further: more
importantly, Goldberg's second Uncle Barney speech went
[p. 38]: the anecdote of his wife calling him in for 'The nicest
piece of rollmop' went [p. 69]: most of the antiphony of Act
Three was cut [pp. 92–3], and most glaring of all, the extensive
dialogue with Lulu just before Stanley's re-entry was entirely
removed. Pinter thus excised Jewish anecdotage that
contributed to the pattern of repetition in the play, removed the
theatrical antiphony that also had a patterned relationship
with the interrogation, and entirely altered the emotional
response to Stanley's re-entry by removing Lulu and all the
strained theatrical laughter of the dialogue. All strengthened
the naturalism of the film by removing elements that derived
from the stage.

   A brief example of the shift in emphasis: Goldberg's wife
apparently called him in for the rollmop herring and pickled
cucumber 'before it gets cold' [p. 69]. Whoever heard of a hot
rollmop? Goldberg's contempt lies in the fact that he assumes
no one present would have any idea, a peculiarly inverted
prejudice. In the film Pinter added a congratulation from
Goldberg as he ascends the stairs to look over his room: 'I bet
you're a baleboosteh' he declares, to Meg's puzzlement – 'A
What?' Goldberg does not bother to explain the Yiddish for an
excellent housekeeper, hardly Meg's case as the camera has
shown us. This addition is less complex and oblique than the
implications of the above omission. The effect of the alterations
strikingly reversed aspects of the presentation of Goldberg.
Tafler's reminiscence of 'Uncle Barney' [pp. 37–8] and 'my old

mum' [p. 53] became a genuine sentimental reverie underlined by close-up which emphasised introspection, exactly paralleling Stanley. This psychological stress is quite different from the subversive theatrical mode which satirically suggests the opposite. Anecdotal music-hall playing, in this context, emphasises role-playing and sentimental idealisation, implying a less cosy reality than the affirmation of family values, which we see later in Goldberg's near breakdown before McCann.

Wigless here in the film, Magee's gleaming cranium was a threat in itself, particularly in the way his head was aggressively thrust forward (not unlike Pringle's Stanley in the 1964 production). Counterpointing Meg's repertoire of gestures, Magee used a concentrated economy of facial expressions – pathological moroseness, baleful lugubriousness, intense tight-lipped cruelty. The Northern Irish rasp exactly complemented the papertearing (used as a sound-over during the opening shots) of Act Two, which was painfully long-drawn out with an unnerving amplification complementing Magee's manic concentration. When McCann says 'Don't touch me' [p. 52] to Stanley, Magee savagely delivered a painful karate chop down on Stanley's arm; and when he says 'I'll kick the shite out of him' [p. 57] the intensity of Magee, visibly shaking with anger as he seized a chair, surging towards the camera, was chilling. The whistling contest between McCann and Stanley was dropped in the film, but the strained awareness of impending catastrophe was there in McCann's drinking at the party. Full tumblers of whisky were down in a single habitual gulp – tongue half out, prepared, the hand delivering the liquor in a sweep to the mouth, anticipating the 'blind' Irish juggernaut in the party game sweeping bottles to the floor and breaking up anything in his way, as he stumbles towards Stanley.

Alan Brien, reviewing Kevin Billington's 1975 production, with Tony Doyle as McCann, considered that 'McCann, the Irish inquisitor, sometimes has been in danger of overbalancing the brain-washing scenes – especially when played by Patrick Magee'. However, 'Here Tony Doyle is always clearly No. 2 yet he manages to encapsulate a coiled, spring-heel violence, all the more disturbing for being under

painful control' (*New Statesman*, 17 January 1975). The realism
of this direction underplayed the humour and, unlike the film,
used restraint in McCann's papertearing. The whistling
contest was used with John Alderton's Stanley aggressively
matching McCann. Goldberg and McCann were often
compared to T. S. Eliot's Eumenides, as Irving Wardle
recalled 'I have seen them played like Furies out of *The Family
Reunion*' but conforming to the 'unemphatic style . . . here it is
simply the arrival of two gentlemen out of season' (*Guardian*, 9
January 1976). This was very much the effect in the film. Given
Billington's style Sydney Tafler's performance fitted
consistently with the cast: no theatrical subversion here, 'there
is never a touch of falsity about his respectable bearing' (*The
Financial Times*, 9.1.75).

'Sure I'm sure' [p. 37] are almost Goldberg's first words, yet
Harold Pinter's portrayal, in Kenneth Ives's production,
belied that confidence throughout the play. Unlike Tafler, in
saying these words his face showed apprehensiveness. As a
young man Pinter occasionally helped out friends by working
as a 'shouter' to draw customers to a stall selling bargains in
Oxford Street. Goldberg recalls that he 'used to be in the
business' [p. 63] of the rag-trade, and the Jewish trader –
cajoling an audience, putting something over, putting on a
show with licensed extravagance – was part of Pinter's
brilliant, complex portrayal. Yet the very gestures in the
confident presentation of a public self were those which
betrayed an inner uneasiness. Pinter's Goldberg constantly
adjusted his clothing – lapel, tie, cuffs, belt – as he constantly
adjusted his accent and his smile. Clearly this major
interpretation took the fact of Goldberg's near breakdown in
Act Three as the emergence of a condition that was subtlely
hinted at throughout, the exact opposite of Tafler's gregarious
Jewish suavity where breakdown seemed a singular aberrance.
Pinter continually suggested a devious personage using the
overbearing loudness of the heavy East End persona
provisionally. In acceding to McCann's request for
information about the 'job' – 'The main issue is a singular issue'
[p. 40] – Pinter's accent was formally bureaucratic, more the
executive within the 'organization' than street trader here.

Similarly Goldberg's acidulous smile was more like a sneer masquerading as a smile.

In a section missing from the film when Goldberg explains to Petey his discussion with a friend about another 'case' of breakdown [p. 82], the apprehensiveness and insecurity grew until, with mention of the Abdullah cigarettes, Pinter became quite disorientated and unable to recall the other brand. The 'case' evidently applied to himself as he is aware and as we saw when he eventually broke before McCann's tearing the paper with a shout that was almost a scream, 'Stop doing that!' [p. 85]. The camera emphasised this by dwelling on Pinter's distress before his eruption. This whole sequence, culminating in the *Vacant, Desperate, Lost* vacuity of BECAUSE I BELIEVE THAT THE WORLD [p. 98], strengthens the parallel with Stanley in the structure of the play. Stanley's attack on the matriarch as embodiment of home is paralleled by inversion in the emptiness of Goldberg recalling his father and Uncle Barney. With McCann's evident dismay in the same act, Ives showed how there were not simply victim and persecutors, but all were vulnerable under the ordinance of 'the hierarchy, the Establishment, the arbiters, the socio-religious monsters' (*Letter to Peter Wood*).

Pat Magee cannot be outdone in the part of McCann in his own style and Colin Blakely did not try to. His McCann was understated and restrained, a gaping automaton, an Ulster sphinx of stone-like antipathy. In fact such a soured mask made a perfect contrast with Pinter's mobile features. As with the face, so with the body, Blakely maintained a permanent hunch, ready to absorb blows, ready to wade in. Such restraint paid off well in the last act when McCann, visibly unnerved by whatever had taken place in Stanley's room in the night, began to lose control. Magee could add nothing here, it had all been given earlier. Blakely's restraint gone, his dismay was quite beyond the querulousness of Act One and was thus absolutely consonant with Ives's control of the third act, and his overview of the play as a whole.

8 *THE CARETAKER*

Mick

Alan Bates, Donald Pleasance and Peter Woodthorpe as, respectively, Mick, Davies and Aston, in the first production of *The Caretaker*, gave possibly the most highly acclaimed ensemble performance of modern times on the British stage. So powerful was it, in fact, that a London revival did not appear until 1972.

In *The Caretaker* the theatrical element we have seen in *The Birthday Party* appears in two modes. The bag-passing game is a stock piece of clowning and was done either in formal grouping with a stylised rhythm or attempted naturalistically, according to the emphasis of each production. However, theatricality is there in some of Davies's utterances, either as a comic relation or one-liner, and in the character of Mick it is internalised and subsumed by the individual. In the first stage production of 1960 Alan Bates's Mick, except for a few crucial moments, presented a front, an ironic posture which in the famous long speeches of Act Two take the form of comic monologues reminiscent of such figures as Dan Leno and Arthur English, as Peter Davison has shown (see Macmillan Casebook). Theatricality is part of Mick's character, part of his defensive and offensive posture (like Goldberg's) to contain and relieve the anger that finally bursts through in Act Three when he smashes the Buddha. Comparing Harold Pinter's stand-in performance as Mick with Alan Bates's, *The Times* reviewer felt that though he lacked 'the tense mercurial worldliness brought in as some relief to the atmosphere of defeat' by Bates, Pinter nevertheless supplied 'a brooding sarcasm which carries its own kind of threat' (21 February 1961). 'Mercurial' aptly characterised Bates's brilliant, indelible performance: volatile, eloquent, deceptively witty.

Alan Bates very much exploited the variety of accent implied in the text which exactly matched his natural range, delivering his 'monologues' in a speedy, clipped, flat London accent, without any particularly heavy cockney tones. This was varied by the constant recourse to sardonic 'posh' pronunciation ('It's awfully nice to meet you' [p. 39]). Such variation, from the politely mannered to the aggressively mannerless, though intimidating and inscrutable for Davies, was very revealing to the audience. In the revised text of 1962 Pinter added Mick's sardonic invitation 'You must come up and have a drink some time. Listen to some Tchaikovsky' [p. 73]. The comic improbability invariably draws laughter in performance, yet Mick is unconsciously giving voice to the mode of existence to which he aspires and which he knows is ultimately beyond him. The penthouse speech [p. 69] is crucial to this. Bates dropped his mordant wryness of tone and began the speech slightly playfully yet with a kind of speculative seriousness, thoughtfully recreating the attic in his own mind which, as the specifications accumulate, gives in to the dream. 'You could put the dining-room across the landing, see?' Here it became apparent that quickened by the modish sophistication succeeding postwar austerity, Mick's purely imaginative engagement had gone well beyond practical possibilities to verbal picture-painting. Aspiration and self-delusion were confounded, and Bates's Mick knew it. When he smashed the Buddha it was not simply out of frustration and anger at the failure of Davies or Aston as interior decorators, but as an oblique acknowledgement of the disparity between his own aspiration and his accomplishment. The first stage direction, following this action read, *To himself, slowly, broodingly*, which Pinter altered to *Passionately*, thereby dropping Mick's protective ironic guise and revealing his actual situation as the reverse of the protestations of his following speech: not a would-be West End architect-interior decorator presiding over an established business, but a suburban jobbing builder, a one-man-band owner of an old van and a brokendown slum. In the 1964 film version the camera emphasised this disparity by cutting from Mick's face to inspect the hopelessly dilapidated walls and kitchen. One added visual image said it all, Mick's van; old, tiny and battered.

In the film version Donald Pleasance reappeared as Davies while Robert Shaw, who succeeded Peter Woodthorpe in New York, took Aston's part. Using the same actors led to the view that the film duplicated the stage performance. For instance, John Russell Taylor, although recognising textual cuts, nevertheless felt that 'the correspondence of effect between play and film is remarkable' (*Sight and Sound*, Winter 1963–64). On the other hand 'It is in fact arguable that *The Caretaker*, however unconventional as a film subject, is even better suited to the realistic means of the cinema than to the more artificial medium of the stage' (*Financial Times*, 13 March 1964). Again, while acknowledging the success of the film, John Coleman confessed his initial qualms: 'It was hard to see how a camera was going to re-create or stand in for the breathing actuality of the theatrical moment' (*New Statesman*, 13 March 1964). Such views are only seemingly opposed. Some aspects of stage and screen corresponded, the screenplay deliberately adapted the play to the realism of the medium which did not attempt to reproduce that 'breathing actuality' of the theatre.

With Bates's screen performance Pinter halved the celebrated speeches of Act Two [pp. 40, 41, 44–5]: the first speech cut out 'Had a marvellous stop-watch . . .' to 'It was a funny business'; the second cut 'This chap . . . to the Nag's Head'; the third 41-line speech has 23 lines cut, including the lengthy final passage 'On the other hand . . . won't we?' What Pinter did was to reduce considerably the theatrical nature of the speeches. The provenance of the speeches in stage monologue is recognised not only in delivery but by the accumulation of detail as the speech continues. It was precisely the conventional monologue details of affiliation and relationship which were excised in the first and second speeches, while in the third the quick-fire staccato of music hall in the closing legalese was entirely removed. The style of the original, uncut speeches needed projecting to a theatre audience. Alan Bates quite masterfully suggested the music-hall tempo and delivery, evoking the worlds of popular entertainment, of parlour, pub or club – evoking that sociable world from which Davies is excluded. In the film subtextual implication was replaced by close-up.

With the evasive comings and goings of Mick after the long-drawn-out opening, the camera repeatedly held his face still in close-up and what we saw was quite different from the face presented to Davies, or Mick's face on stage. When alone, or unseen by the others, Mick's face showed troubled concern, something daunted by a hurt that time had not erased but hardened, the obverse of Mick's public mask of acerbic neutrality, the mask largely maintained in the theatre. This came to the surface in one of the most powerful lines in the film performance which can go unnoticed in the text. Mick actually says very little at all to his brother. Most of the time he will not, or cannot, confront Aston, until they come face to face in Act Two. A drip into the bucket breaks a lengthy silence and then Mick says 'You still got that leak!' In this simple observation Bates packed the mixed emotions of a fraught, long-term relationship. Caught partly offguard, his Mick could not say what he felt and perhaps doesn't himself know the meaning of his own feelings. His tone hesitantly attempted sarcasm but the weight of feeling broke through into a compounded appeal and protest – resentment, hope, frustration, love, anxiety and bewilderment. Bates recovered himself and in the following exchange maintained his old sardonic self until the end of the bag-passing game which follows, when he hung his head, biting his lip, in unwitting resignation to Aston's condition and all that it implies. Alan Bates's Mick was so evasive because what he really avoided was his own incapacity to confront honestly Aston's condition, caught between the conflicting impulses of social rejection of the aberrant and personal feelings for a brother.

One of the great ironies of Pinter's plays in general is that in proportion to the absence of explanation for motive the auditor's intuition is called on to reconstruct psychologically the underlying cause of behaviour, and this behaviour depends on the particular emphases decided on by actor and director. Where motivation itself is psychologically ambivalent, then once again we find another kind of precarious balance which calls for a correspondingly sensitive response. Bates's performance was richly ambivalent indeed, as I have tried to indicate, but the critics' simplified interpretation of an unuttered bond of fraternal love was often voiced. The *New Yorker* reported that Mick though 'cynical' and 'cruel' was bound to Aston 'by a fiercely protective devotion' (9 July 1960). There was a complexity in Bates's performance beyond the melodramatic reversal of this rather one-dimensional view. John Hurt's portrayal of Mick in 1972 was also seen in these terms, a possessive 'protection of his brother's dignity'

(*Observer*, 5 March 1972). Christopher Morahan's direction came 'as a welcome contrast to the monumental Pinter, with its statuesque poise and marble surfaces, as laid down by Peter Hall's productions' (*Times*, 3 March 1972). Irving Wardle continued with a pointed contrast 'John Hurt's Mick dispenses crafty mobility rather than the saturnine power which Alan Bates brought to the part. Instead of brooding over the house, he plays as equal partner in the trio'. Turning from the studied postures of '60s productions, Morahan's was characterised by 'a broadly comic style' (*Daily Mirror*, 3 March 1972). As a consequence 'The mood has mellowed. Gone is the sinister touch. These fellows, for all their boasting, would not hurt a fly. And gone is the brooding sense of sadness as they try to talk to each other' (*Evening News*, 3 March 1972). Where Alan Bates made even the most innocent dialogue palpably menacing, John Hurt's performance showed only an 'equivocal chumminess' (*Guardian*, 3 March 1972).

The need for a perceptible stress in the direction of Mick was just what was found lacking in Kevin Billington's 1976 version, 'Nor does the production cast any light on the one enigma of the plot . . . What does Mick, the watchful arbitrator want? From Simon Rouse's performance, it seems that all he wants is to play sadistic games with the old man' (*Times*, 7 April 1976). In contrast to Alan Bates's constant irony which suggested a deflected psychological complexity, Simon Rouse's Mick was 'played . . . as a houseproud dreamer who genuinely hopes for [Davies's] cooperation' (*New Statesman*, 23 April 1976). Antony Higgins played Mick the following year in Paul Joyce's production at Greenwich which was paced extremely slowly, running for over three hours. Where Alan Bates's delivery of the penthouse speech contrasted with Aston's slow pace, Higgins's Mick lingered 'lovingly over his vision of the redecorated hovel at the expense of achieving the contrast in tempo with the slow-thinking Aston' (*Times*, 25 October 1977). So powerful was Bates's performance that inevitably it became the unstated standard by which successors were judged: 'Higgins . . . lacks that element of saturnine menace and dangerous jokeyness that should be a constant threat to the tramp' (*Times*, 25 October 1977).

When the National Theatre honoured Pinter's 50th birthday

in 1980 with a production of *The Caretaker* (which transferred to
TV the following year) reviews welcomed the clarity of
conception in the portrayal of Mick by Jonathan Pryce.
'Kenneth Ives seems in his direction to have settled on the view
of the play as the story of Mick's attempt to re-establish contact
with his brother, using any means at his disposal. Davies
therefore becomes a useful tool, because it is he who has
somehow managed to revive, in however rudimentary a form,
Aston's desire to make contact with the world outside' (John
Russell Taylor, *Drama*, no 140, 1981). The penthouse speech
crystallised Pryce's motive. Gone is Bates's self-conscious edge
that deflected finely balanced self-delusion and self-derision
into the breathtaking catalogue which contemptuously
stupefies Davies. 'For once, his fantasy of transforming the
house into a colour-supplement paradise is not a joke. He
delivers it, lying flat on his back, as a reverie; only coming to
when Davies asks who will be living there, and gets the answer
"my brother and me" ' (*Times*, 12 November 1980). In the film
Pinter gave Aston the additional line 'It's got possibilities'
contrasting his credulousness with Mick's underlying
recognition of the fantasy. Eileen Diss's set in 1980 was
consistent with Pryce's delivery of the penthouse speech. The
first production and the film emphasised the claustrophobia of
the attic 'but the wide stage of the Lyttelton allowed, if it did not
force, Eileen Diss's set to spread out into something which
might possibly, with work done on it, turn into a desirable
residence'. Consistent with this was Pryce's unremitting
naturalism. Modifying Harry H. Corbett's idiolect in Galton
and Simpson's *Steptoe and Son*, Pryce's heavy cockney delivery
was unwaveringly true: no playfulness here and more totally
saturnine than mercurial. The theatrical stage monologue
aspect of the Act Two speeches was reinterpreted
naturalistically, as if Davies actually did remind him of his
uncle's brother, as Pryce nodded agreement with his own
observation. Naturalism came under strain here, Pryce's active
amazement saved 'married a Chinaman and went to Jamaica'
but the line 'day after they chucked him out of the Salvation
Army' [p. 40] could not survive naturalistic delivery, for all
Pryce's brilliance. Ironically, this interpretation did have a
major gain. When Bates's Mick suggested that he was

'straightforward' [p. 70] to Davies, the irony was hilarious, but when Pryce said it he meant it. Bates's exploitation of the theatrical temporarily enlisted the audience on his side: for Pryce the only audience was Davies. Pryce's insistent literalness made his vacillating view of Davies all the more warped, and thus the latent violence was all the more fearful and precarious. Bates's playful Mick needed Davies to despise, otherwise, alone, he would despise himself, whereas Pryce needed his brother, a frustrated need which, in the close-up of television, brought him almost to tears after he smashes the Buddha. Bates gave a subtlely manifold, psychologically suggestive performance, Pryce had a singular intensity.

Aston

The part of Aston is the most difficult in the play. The characters of Mick and Davies necessarily have a variety of gestures – vocal and physical – but Aston, partially numbed by his experience in a mental hospital, just has the toaster and the odd plank to occupy him. Peter Woodthorpe's genius, in the first production, lay in the recognition that the actor had to be true to the stunned quality of Aston's behaviour and not to try and do more with the part than the script indicated. Harold Hobson accordingly responded to the performance, the 'first achievement' of the play was Woodthorpe's Aston, 'extraordinarily formidable . . . a latent implacability . . . so powerful and so quiet' (*Sunday Times*, 5 June 1960). The oddity of Woodthorpe's Aston came from within, inevitably, as a total condition, not an occasional aberration provoked by something external. Aston's stillness was like a grotesque travesty of the statue of the Buddha he has brought to the attic, as his long speech closing Act Two makes manifest. 'The finest single speech . . . heard in a long time . . . the terrors are at last spoken' (*New Statesman*, 7 May 1960). The 'fine groping pathos' (*Financial Times*, 28 April 1960) was 'the very reverse of sensational . . . in delivering it Mr Woodthorpe never raises his voice, but his variations in tone are of infinite subtlety' (*Sunday Times*, 5 June 1960). As Pinter has pointed out, we do not have

to believe all that Aston says here. Whatever the precise reality was, it is now refracted through Aston's damaged mind.
Robert Shaw took a different approach. He recognised that the more normal he attempted to be as Aston, the more painfully contrasted his manifest oddity would be. 'Robert Shaw is, in both manner and appearance, surprisingly normal . . . Peter Woodthorpe had an odder, more offbeat appearance, and he did more to play up the character's eccentricities' (*Times*, 15 November 1961). This rather belied the effect of Shaw's closely cropped head which appeared 'a forehead that would seem to have been fashioned of concrete' (*New York Herald Tribune*, 5 October 1961). This visual feature contrasted fearfully with the apparent 'normality', particularly so in the film where the camera movement was aptly exploited. The very low ceiling and sloping roof of the location attic often forced the characters into a crowded position which was duplicated by Nicolas Roeg's camera. Angled shots repeatedly emphasised the claustrophobia, with characters occasionally pressing their heads not only against the ceiling but up into the camera frame itself. Roeg's camera moved with a caged wariness giving expression to the suppressed feelings of the characters. During Aston's long speech the camera, closing in all the time, took different positions warily looking down on Aston, in profile, slowly to full face, and so on, cutting twice to Davies listening, quite still. All the time we are brought closer and closer to that powerful threatening forehead, with Ron Grainer's atmospheric sound effect of hollow tapping heightening our sense of the danger of such strength of body with such fragility of mind.
With the film version of Aston, as with that of Mick, Pinter particularly modified a passage which had strong theatrical association with the materials of the revue sketch. This was the sequence of exchanges on the saws [p. 33]. As with Pinter's sketch 'Trouble in the Works' the comedy lies partly in transferring the terminology of a specialist milieu to the stage: in the sketch the toolmaker's workshop, in the play to a carpenter's equipment. In the first performance of 1960–61 this was quite extensive, and remarked on by some reviewers. Aston and Davies's exchanges concerned a jig-saw, fret saw, hacksaw, keyhole saw and the efficacy of a portable drill. With

publication of the revised text of 1962, references were reduced to the simple exchange on the jig-saw and Aston's explanation about its 'family' relationship with the fret saw. Obviously Pinter came to feel that it was overwritten and tipped the balance too heavily towards unalloyed comedy. With the screenplay, all mention of the saws in the passage went, only 'portable drill' remained, replacing the first mention of a jig-saw. In addition, the following anecdote of the woman in the café who wanted to look at Aston's body has been excised. With the sombre black, white and grey of celluloid, and the winter reality of Hackney, it was realised that some humour would have the wrong emphasis – more part of a theatrical rhythm and pace, than that of the cinema.

Peter Woodthorpe had the almost haunted vacancy of someone immersed in the inner world of self and the past, whereas in 1972 'In comparison with the original version, the Mermaid performance was externalized' (*Times*, 3 March 1972). Jeremy Kemp's performance had a clarity and intelligibility that missed a fundamental aspect of Aston: 'Mr Kemp's superficially lucid handling of the lines and pauses conveys little of the dislocated thought processes behind them' (*Times*, 3 March 1972). Roger Lloyd Pack, as Aston in 1976, was directed to keep within areas of the stage, 'Mr Billington's stage picture makes it clear that the characters relate to their environment in different ways . . . Each member of the cast thus inhabits the space in his own way' (*Times*, 7 April 1976). Lloyd Pack made the business of the toaster, accommodating Davies, and sandpapering the plank, practical and mechanical props performed 'in a manner wholly drained of feeling' (*Times*, 7 April 1976). On the other hand, Peter Guinness in 1977 gave expression to a vestigial pain in his long speech, and, as against Lloyd Pack's use of space, used his body, 'hanging his head as though he had broken his neck' (*Sunday Times*, 30 October 1977) and moving with 'a tortoise-like gait' (*Observer*, 30 October 1977). The two contrasting images that remain of these two performances are the bowed stillness of Peter Guinness remotely oblivious to Davies's anecdotes and the intensity of Lloyd Pack's involvement with his jobs. With this variety of approaches to such a seemingly limited part it would seem rather difficult to find further aspects of character for reinterpretation, but this Kenneth Ives did with a powerful simplicity in 1980.

Aston picked up the Buddha because it 'looked quite nice' and was 'very well made' [pp. 26–7]. Davies tells Mick later that when he was supposedly asleep he spied on Aston smiling down on him. Anticipating the faint smiles of Act Three, Kenneth Ives saw the cues here for a comprehensive reinterpretation of Aston. Intermittently, throughout the play, Kenneth Cranham's Aston, like the Buddha, sat upright with a faint smile on his face. Cranham, unlike predecessors, had a sense of calmness as if the tasks that lay ahead – the shed, the roof, the decoration – had provided a rationale to contemplate. When he smilingly attended to the electric plug in Act One it was as if it were an object of meditation that had brought peace. In the television version, Ives used a rather dominant statue of Buddha much larger than usual, and had it constantly brought into focus as a presiding spirit which Aston almost ritualistically acknowledged by repeatedly paying attention to it. The Buddha for Cranham was the symbol of hope for the future, turning Aston's back on the past and its suffering and aggression. In this production Davies came to represent that past in the renewed persecution of Aston. In his long speech Cranham showed in the final words of intention how he had displaced feelings of revenge. When Davies jibed at his 'stinking shed' [p. 77] this was Aston's test, but rather than give in to violence he controlled his anger and turned the word back on Davies, which was exactly what Mick wanted to hear when Davies reported it to him, 'I? Stink! You hear that?' [p. 79]. This prepared the emotional ground for the encounter of Mick and Aston and their mutual smiles.

This smile is the litmus test for productions of the play. A director must intuitively apprehend the subtext here by thinking through the whole play sensing the oblique relationship between surface and substratum in and between each brother. In the first production Peter Woodthorpe's smile was visibly there, as was Mick's in response, but it remained ambiguous. '*Both are smiling, faintly*' [p. 84] is Pinter's stage direction. In the film as Aston entered he was directly beside Mick who smiled first, in profile. Robert Shaw's response was barely perceptible. The cutting of dialogue from the opening of

Act Three excised the knowledge that Aston had actually done something – tarred the roof. In the first production the smile indicates that Aston was agreeing with Mick's view of the situation, and of Davies in particular. Ironically, Pinter felt that the film had greater clarity in foregrounding psychological ambiguity and getting rid of circumstantial ambiguity with the actual house and the reality of London. In the film the smile deepened ambiguity, it did not resolve it. Bates's 'Look . . . uh . . .' which followed, had an emotional frankness, yet the precise nature of such frankness was curtailed by the broken utterance. However, the restraint of Shaw here indicated the troubled continuation of a disturbed mind, with or without Davies. In complete contrast, when Cranham entered he smiled openly and unambiguously: Mick responded, and when the camera returned to Cranham's face he grinned broadly in happy, affectionate brotherhood. Mick's smile was reinforced by emphatic relief compensating for his distress a moment earlier. But it must be noted that this goes directly against the stage direction. With Kenneth Ives's direction it was as if Cranham's smile throughout had been awaiting the right time to manifest itself in a mutual realisation and attachment, as it did here with Mick, in restoration and renewal. Together.

Davies

Donald Pleasance was a very well-established actor, nationally known for his television work, before the advent of *The Caretaker*, but with his portrayal of Davies during two years in London and New York, followed by the film, he gave one of the finest performances in living memory. The word performance itself seemed inadequate, the 'Dickensian richness' seemed 'more of an incarnation than an impersonation' (*Sunday Express*, 15 March 1964). Indeed John Cutts felt of all of the actors that 'Rather than three performances three *existences* are given' (*Films and Filming*, January 1964). The text remains as an ossified inscription to the life that was the part, where words were part of gesture. Selecting Pleasance for the West End's top performance, Robert Muller paid tribute to the way every single detail contributed towards a total impact that was both personally felt and true to the playwright's intention. 'Watch how Mr. Pleasance quickly sketches the man after his first entrance: the frostbitten hands, half-covered with shreds of mitten, jabbing the air with empty malevolence, or hitching up his trousers, the fingers compulsively scratching under his waistcoat.' Every vocal or physical gesture was an expression of fundamental characteristics, even when caught out by the unexpected: 'Observe the doltish look of guilty enchantment as he is given a crisp white sheet to sleep on, a look more eloquent than a whole act of exposition'. Suspiciousness, self-assertion and arrogance 'are reflected in the hunched shoulders, the furtive loping step, the Napoleonic stance when he is mentioned, the chewing mouth, the sudden feverish scratch over the back of one hand, the threat of work fearfully swimming in his eyes, the hopeful gloss spreading over his face when he is provided with a handsome red smoking-jacket' (*Daily Mail*, 2 August 1960).

When, in the film, Mick offered Davies a sandwich, Pleasance laughed with a childish innocent glee that was totally disarming. This Davies ate repulsively as though his teeth were half missing or loose, with the food at the front of the mouth. But that laugh, like the expressions noted by Muller when something was unexpectedly given Davies, complicated response. Pleasance's Davies was wholly repellent. Filthy and smelling, he blew his nose into his fingers. He was servile and selfish with a continual whining rasp of voice, yet we cannot entirely reject such nastiness. We cannot separate the character from his condition. For all his protestations he is so vulnerable. As a person he is loathsome, but to loathe simply him would be to abrogate our moral response to his condition. All along this moral response is deferred by laughter. On stage and in the film Pleasance sat down several times lifting his filthy overcoat as though he were a concert pianist in tails. Such ludicrously misplaced decorum had a richly burlesque element which elicited derision rather than sympathy. That derision had to be emotionally paid for at the close.

As we have seen with Mick and Aston, Pinter modified dialogue to adjust the humour to suit the film medium. Comedy was still there but it was considerably less uproarious than stage performance. It was equally and necessarily so with

Davies since the film immediately made apparent the harsh physical reality of a tramp's life: on the road, in the snow, at night, in sandals. On stage the more immediate reality was that Davies had got himself sacked for refusing to do his job. Accordingly, Pleasance varied his delivery in the two media. On stage the Luton speech was comically paced around 'Piss off, he said to me . . . If you don't piss off, he says . . . piss off out of it' [p. 23]. In the film the camera combined with Davies's movements to break up completely the narrative rhythm of the story: the monk's words, rather than being projected to a live audience and thus accommodating subsequent laughter, were actually understated. Davies's comic volley to Mick's 'That's my mother's bed' – 'Well she wasn't in it last night' [p. 44] evoked the world of music hall and the double act, but in the film it was delivered quite naturalistically, quietly, with trepidation. Again the psychological displaced the theatrical and Pleasance thoroughly trained himself for this by adopting the 'method' acting discipline which saw him begging on the streets of Hackney between takes.

A playwright cannot supply completely exhaustive stage directions. The dialogue itself suggests gesture. In *The Caretaker* Pinter did supply a key mannerism at the outset 'DAVIES *exclaims loudly, punches downward with closed fist*' [p. 17], but thereafter director and actor must intuitively work out the details – as with Pleasance's raised coat tails. The social implication of this gesture, which might well have been prompted from Davies's protestation 'I've had dinner with the best' [p. 18], was developed in the two productions of 1972 and 1977 by Leonard Rossiter and Max Wall. Rossiter transferred the physical gesture into a vocal inflection, 'In his voice there are traces of an educated accent that make you wonder if he did indeed once "have dinner with the best" ' (*Daily Mail*, 3 March 1972). Though mostly characterised by a much travelled Welsh accent, Pleasance had developed a mongrel voice with occasionally odd flat Midlands tones breaking through, as if time and place had worn away the originally identifying accent he wished to hide anyway. It appears that he, the bigot, had been at the receiving end of prejudice (he will not confirm his Welsh background and thinks of himself as 'an Englishman to pour their tea' [see pp. 34, 36]). In 1972 'Shedding the remembered Pleasance inflections Rossiter'[s] ... voice constantly aspires to pseudo-gentility' (*Guardian*, 3 March 1972). Pleasance's performance was an 'incarnation' rather than an 'impersonation' and it was a difficult act to follow, 'Leonard Rossiter's tramp at first seemed dangerously close to a twitching, scratching impersonation of Donald Pleasance's original'. And yet again the class emphasis was recognised as an essential reinterpretation, 'but he soon stamps it with a genteel, grotesque quality all his own' (*Observer*, 5 March 1972). This carried the risk that all you were left with was just that, a theatrical grotesque, and Rossiter pushed it to its limits 'through applied physical and vocal mannerisms which project the full grotesqueness of the man but leave you aware of a consciousness producing something grotesque' (*Times*, 3 March 1972). For example, the fame of the Luton speech as a comic setpiece led Rossiter's delivery to surrender entirely to the posture of telling an established joke. However, Rossiter rescued the role partly by finding a range of gesture suitable for his gangling frame as against Pleasance's shortness. He gave the impression of an angular bird-like scavenger, 'an old raven ... He croaks and caws and flaps his way through the night' (*Illustrated London News*, May 1972); 'a cawing, predatory scarecrow-figure' (*Guardian*, 3 March 1972). Rossiter particularly used his arms in nervy twitching, and jutting out, a mannerism used to devastating effect when 'closing in on the brain-damaged Aston with his arms converted into pincer-like electrodes' (*Times*, 3 March 1972). Rossiter was a highly mannered comic actor with a distinct style which took the part to 'the naturalism of the grotesque' to use Robert Brustein's description of the play (*Seasons of Discontent*). An advantage of Rossiter's performance was its 'clarity of outline' which 'in the end ... with his cracked servile smile and scrapheap body, does touch the heart of the play' (*Times*, 3 March 1972).

Max Wall, like the other music-hall comedians Jimmy Jewel and Arthur English, successfully extended his later career in the 'straight' theatre. As Davies, like Rossiter, he affected 'a grotesquely genteel accent' (*Times*, 25 October 1977), but unlike his predecessor, he did not find a range of gesture. Instead, from the outset, he struck an unwavering correlative to the accent in a dignified pose. As Michael Billington commented 'his speciality as an actor is a frayed, benign dignity' (*Guardian*, 25 October 1977). Max Wall converted the role to his characteristic range rather than attempting to extend his range to equal the role. Wall looked and sounded the part with war medals, stringbound overcoat and his strikingly worn face and gravelly voice, yet so much of Davies was missing: malice, shiftiness, ingratiation and self-assertion were all lacking. There was no sense of that unfolding disclosure of facets of character by an accumulation of detail as Pleasance gave, structured round the principle of oscillation which shapes the play. Donald Pleasance's performance was so comprehensive that Rossiter and Wall were forced to find alternative possibilities, and as a consequence both took as literal possibility the ludicrous gesture of past gentility from a man who also boasts friendship with a Shepherd's Bush lavatory attendant. The danger of such satirical presentation of Davies lies in its concession to a theatrical typology of the hypocrite, with its diametrical polarisation of tramp/gentleman rather than the complex balance of a more compounded character.

Surprisingly, a performance that seemed to go directly against the text and yet succeeded, was that of the Scottish actor Fulton Mackay in Kevin Billington's 1976 production. Mackay did not try to convert his natural accent. No gentility here and none of Pleasance's Davies, 'a man from nowhere . . . always blurring the edges with his anomalous voice': instead, inflecting his voice Mackay was 'palpably a Glaswegian down-and-out, with the rolling bully's walk, the cajoling mouth to the ear and the beggar's hand turned sideways for a handout' (*Times*, 7 April 1976). He was 'no cringing Welsh cadge, but a once-vigorous, still canny Glaswegian-on-the-make' (*New Statesman*, 23 April 1976). The portrayal, it was noted, even survived unchanged Davies's aside on 'that Scotch git' [p. 19]. More importantly, this assertive and aggressive conception made the power struggle between Davies and Mick less unbalanced, shifting the sense of a long-term strategy of ownership and disownment from Rouse's merely sadistic Mick onto Davies. Here Davies's servility seemed less an occasional recourse than part of a larger plan: 'there seems to be a crafty intelligence behind the camouflage and the big nocturnal assault on Aston seems premeditated from the start' (*Times*, 7 April 1976).

Kenneth Ives's direction of Davies directly challenged that of 1960 since he based his conception on no one particular trait or gesture of the character but attempted a balanced completeness with Warren Mitchell who gave everything to the part: '. . . what a contained actor he is. There are no stray bits of Warren Mitchell left flapping about at the edges; everything goes into the character' (*Observer*, 16 November 1980). In contrast to Pleasance's mixed voice, Mitchell opted for a South Wales valleys accent which was consistently and convincingly maintained. But like Pleasance, some of the gestures devised by Mitchell were integral to the part as a whole. Following through Pinter's pugilistic stage direction Davies here, particularly in the first act, frequently emitted a compressed 'pah!' combined with an upward gesture of his arm, a punch and a stab that ends as a gesture warding off something. Threat ended in defence. Again, the gesture of punching his fist into his hand ended as an open hand rubbing against the other. Similarly, the squaring up motion of the shoulders was the same as the hunching of the shoulders against the cold. These details suggested the core of Davies here – more acted upon than acting, more the victim of circumstance than maker of his own situation. The physical repellence of Pleasance's Davies combined with a constitutional nastiness made him seem warped by something within. The first production avoided sentimentality at all costs. Ives unashamedly saw an essential innocence that was only turned to viciousness when the possibility of ownership arose in the third act. With Pleasance every look, every gesture assumed an ulterior motive in others, even when bewildered by Mick's monologues. Mitchell was just bewildered, mouth agape. When Mick questions Davies about serving abroad as a soldier, Pleasance's affirmative was to deceive, Mitchell's was simply to comply. Pleasance's face, constantly puzzled and pugnaciously baffled, was nearly always vicious and nasty, evoking laughter at his stupidity. Mitchell's knowing, conspiratorial and collusive gape, tongue lolling, assuming a common ground, was funny and sad in its mistaken simplicity.

By the close both Pleasance and Mitchell's Davies's arrived

at the truth of the play, 'for the truth that lies at the heart of all comic performances is the kernel of pathos' (*Financial Times*, 28 April 1960). Yet Noel Coward thought that the basic premise of *The Caretaker* was 'victory rather than defeat' (*Sunday Times*, 15 January 1961). What grows from the 'kernel', the performance over, develops from 'pathos' into something larger, the recognition that art has a morality beside good or bad, right or wrong, in the validity of its vision and the authenticity of its expression. Davies might well be defeated but the truth of his depiction, the truth that the worthless are not forsaken and the forsaken are not worthless, is the ultimate victory of art.

READING LIST

The standard bibliography is Steven H. Gale *Harold Pinter: An Annotated Bibliography* (Boston, Mass., 1978). The most useful book on these early plays is the Macmillan Casebook devoted to *Harold Pinter: The Birthday Party, The Caretaker and The Homecoming* (London, 1986) edited by Michael Scott which contains general and specific critical articles with some contemporary reviews. General introductory studies are Martin Esslin, *Pinter A Study of His Plays* (London, 1977) and Bernard F. Dukore, *Harold Pinter* (London, 1982). Recent collections of critical essays are Alan Bold (ed.), *Harold Pinter. You Never Heard Such Silence* (London, 1984) and Steven Gale (ed.), *Harold Pinter. Critical Approaches* (London, 1986). David T. Thompson provides a fascinating account of Pinter's early years in the repertory theatre in his *Harold Pinter the Player's Playwright* (London, 1985). William Baker and Stephen Ely Tabachnik's *Harold Pinter* (Edinburgh, 1973) remains useful for its first chapter account of Pinter's early milieu. *Where Laughter Stops: Pinter's Tragicomedy* (London, 1977) by Bernard F. Dukore makes an important contribution in stressing the significance of laughter and seriousness in the structure of Pinter's plays. 'Games' as a fundamental element in Pinter's drama is the subject of Guido Almansi and Simon Henderson's *Harold Pinter* (London, 1983). The most outstanding study of recent years, placing Pinter in a wider intellectual and dramatic context is *The Existential and its Exits: Literary and Philosophical Perspectives in the Work of Beckett, Ionesco, Genet and Pinter* (London, 1986) by L. A. C. Dobrez. *Pinter's Female Portraits* (London, 1987) by E. Sakellaridou contains discussion of Pinter criticism.

INDEX OF NAMES